A Serious

PROPOSAL

to the

LADIES

A Serious

PROPOSAL

to the

LADIES

BY

MARY ASTELL

SOURCE BOOK PRESS

All rights reserved. No part of this book may be reproduced
in any form without permission from the publisher.
Library of Congress Catalogue Card No. 77-134177
ISBN 0-87681-054-7
SOURCE BOOK PRESS, a Division of Collectors Editions Ltd.,
185 Madison Avenue, New York, N.Y. 10016
Unabridged republication of the 1701 London edition: First printing 1970
NOTE ON THE TEXT: For the convenience of the modern reader, obvious
typographical errors in the original edition have been corrected, and
corrections indicated for Part II in the Errata of the original have been made.
Type for this edition has been newly set.
Manufactured in the United States of America

A Serious
PROPOSAL
to the
LADIES

for the
Advancement of their
True and Greatest
INTEREST

BY

MARY ASTELL

PART I.

By a Lover of her SEX

The Fourth Edition

LONDON

Printed by *J.R.* for *R. Wilkin*, at the *King's Head* in *St. Paul's Church-Yard*, MDCCI.

THE
CONTENTS

THE CONTENTS

A Serious

PROPOSAL

to the

LADIES

A Serious
PROPOSAL
TO THE
LADIES.

LADIES,

Since the Profitable Adventures that have gone abroad in the World have met with so great Encouragement, tho' the highest advantage they can propose, is an uncertain Lot for such matters as Opinion, not real worth, gives a value to; things which if obtain'd are as flitting and fickle as that Chance which is to dispose of them; I therefore persuade my self, you will not be less kind to a Proposition that comes attended with more certain and substantial Gain; whose only design is to improve your Charms and heighten your Value, by suffering you no longer to be cheap and contemptible. Its aim is to fix that Beauty, to make it lasting and permanent, which Nature with all the helps of Art cannot secure, and to place it out of the reach of Sickness and Old Age, by transferring it from a corruptible Body to an immortal Mind. An obliging Design, which wou'd procure them *inward* Beauty, to whom Nature has unkindly denied the *outward*, and not permit those Ladies who have comely Bodies, to tarnish their Glory with deformed Souls. Wou'd have you all be Wits, or what is better, Wise. Raise you above the Vulgar by something more truly illustrious, than a sounding Title or a great Estate. Wou'd excite in you a generous Emulation to excel in the best things, and not in such Trifles as every mean person who has but Money enough may purchase as well as you. Not suffer you to take up with the low thought of distinguishing your selves by any thing that is not truly valuable, and procure you such Ornaments as all the Treasures of the *Indies* are not able to purchase. Wou'd help you to surpass the Men as much in Vertue and Ingenuity, as you do in Beauty, that you may not only be as lovely, but as wise as Angels. Exalt and Establish your Fame, more than the best wrought *Poems* and loudest

I

Panegyricks, by ennobling your Minds with such Graces as really deserve it. And instead of the Fustian Complements and Fulsome Flatteries of your Admirers, obtain for you the Plaudit of Good Men and Angels, and the approbation of Him who cannot err. In a word, render you the Glory and Blessing of the present Age, and the Admiration and Pattern of the next. And sure, I shall not need many words to persuade you to close with this *Proposal.* The very offer is a sufficient inducement, nor does it need the set-off's of *Rhetorick* to recommend it, were I capable, which yet I am not, of applying them with the greatest force. Since you can't be so unkind to your selves, as to refuse you *real* Interest, I only entreat you to be so wise as to examine wherein it consists; for nothing is of worse consequence than to be deceiv'd in a matter of so great concern. 'Tis as little beneath your Grandeur as your Prudence, to examine curiously what is in this case offer'd you, and to take care that cheating Hucksters don't impose upon you with deceitful Ware. This is a Matter infinitely more worthy your Debates, than what Colours are most agreeable, or what's the Dress becomes you best. Your *Glass* will not do you half so much service as a serious reflection on your own Minds, which will discover Irregularities more worthy your Correction, and keep you from being either too much elated or depress'd by the Representations of the other. 'Twill not be near so advantageous to consult with your Dancing Master as with your own Thoughts, how you may with greatest exactness tread in the Paths of Vertue, which has certainly the most attractive *Air,* and Wisdom the most graceful and becoming *Mien:* Let these attend you, and your Carriage will be always well compos'd, and ev'ry thing you do will carry its Charm with it. No solicitude in the adornation of your selves is dis-commended, provided you imploy your care about that which is really your *self,* and do not neglect that particle of Divinity within you, which must survive, and may (if you please) be happy and perfect, when it's unsuitable and much inferiour Companion is mouldring into Dust. Neither will any pleasure be denied you, who are only desir'd not to catch at the Shadow and let the Substance go. You may be as ambitious as you please, so you aspire to the best things, and contend with your Neigh-bours as much as you can, that they may not out do you in any commendable Quality. Let it never be said, That they to

2

whom pre-eminence is so very agreeable, can be tamely content that others sho'd surpass them in *this,* and precede them in a *better* World! Remember, I pray you, the famous Women of former Ages, the *Orinda's* of late, and the more Modern Heroins, and blush to think how much is now, and will hereafter be said of them, when you your selves (as great a Figure as you make) must be buried in silence and forgetfulness! Shall your Emulation fail *there only* where 'tis commendable? Why are you so pre-posterously humble, as not to contend for one of the highest Mansions in the Court of Heav'n? Believe me, Ladies, this is the only *Place* worth contending for, you are neither better nor worse in your selves for going before, or coming after *now,* but you are really so much the better, by how much the higher your station is in an Orb of Glory. How can you be content to be in the World like Tulips in a Garden, to make a fine *shew* and be good for nothing; have all your Glories set in the Grave, or perhaps much sooner! What your own sentiments are I know not, but I can't without pity and resentment reflect, that those Glorious Temples on which your kind Creator has bestow'd such exquisite Workmanship, shou'd enshrine no better than *Aegyptian* Deities; be like a garnish'd Sepulchre, which for all its glittering, has nothing within but emptiness or putrefaction! What a pity it is, that whilst your Beauty casts a lustre all around you, your Souls which are infinitely more bright and radiant, (of which if you had but a clear Idea, as lovely as it is, and as much as you now value it, you wou'd then despise and neglect the mean *Case* that encloses it) shou'd be suffer'd to over-run with weeds, lie fallow and neglected, unadorn'd with any Grace! Altho' the Beauty of the mind is necessary to secure those Conquests which your Eyes have gain'd, and Time that mortal Enemy to handsome Faces, has no influence on a lovely Soul, but to better and improve it. For shame let's abandon that *Old,* and therefore one wou'd think, unfashionable employment of pursuing Butter-flies and Trifles! No longer drudge on in the dull beaten road of Vanity and Folly which so many have gone before us, but dare to break the enchanted Circle that custom has plac'd us in, and scorn the Vulgar way of imitating all the Impertinencies of our Neighbours. Let us learn to pride our selves in something more excellent than the invention of a Fashion, and not entertain such a degrading thought of our own

3

worth, as to imagine that our Souls were given us only for the service of our Bodies, and that the best improvement we can make of these, is to attract the Eyes of Men. We value *them* too much, and our *selves* too little, if we place any part of our desert in their Opinion, and don't think our selves capable of Nobler Things than the pitiful Conquest of some worthless heart. She who has opportunities of making an interest in Heaven, of obtaining the love and admiration of GOD and Angels, is too prodigal of her Time, and injurious to her Charms, to throw them away on vain insignificant men. She need not make her self so cheap as to descend to court their Applauses, for at the greater distance she keeps, and the more she is above them, the more effectually she secures their esteem and wonder. Be so generous then, Ladies, as to do nothing unworthy of you; so true to your Interest, as not to lessen your Empire and depreciate your Charms. Let not your Thoughts be wholly busied in observing what respect is paid you, but a part of them at least, in studying to deserve it. And after all, remember that Goodness is the truest Greatness; to be wise for your selves the greatest Wit; and *that* Beauty the most desirable which will endure to Eternity.

Pardon me the seeming rudeness of this Proposal, which goes upon a supposition that there's something amiss in you, which it is intended to amend. My design is not to expose, but to rectifie your Failures. To be exempt from mistake, is a priviledge few can pretend to, the greatest is to be past Conviction and too obstinate to reform. Even the *Men*, as exact as they wou'd seem, and as much as they divert themselves with our Miscarriages, are very often guilty of greater faults, and such, as considering the advantages they enjoy, are much more inexcusable. But I will not pretend to correct their Errors, who either are, or at least *think* themselves too wise to receive Instruction from a Womans Pen. My earnest desire is, That you Ladies, would be as perfect and happy as 'tis possible to be in this imperfect state; for I Love you too well to endure a spot upon your Beauties, if I can by any means remove and wipe it off. I would have you live up to the dignity of your Nature, and express your thankfulness to GOD for the benefits you enjoy by a due improvement of them: As I know very many of you do, who countenance that Piety which the men decry, and are the brightest Patterns

4

of Religion that the Age affords, 'tis my grief that all the rest of our Sex do not imitate such Illustrious Examples, and therefore I would have them encreas'd and render'd more conspicuous, that Vice being put out of countenance, (because Vertue is the only thing in fashion) may sneak out of the World, and its darkness be dispell'd by the confluence of so many shining Graces. The Men perhaps will cry out that I teach you false Doctrin, for because by their deductions some amongst us are become very mean and contemptible, they would fain persuade the rest to be as despicable and forlorn as they. We're indeed oblig'd to them for their management, in endeavouring to make us so, who use all the artifice they can to spoil, and deny us the means of improvement. So that instead of inquiring why all Women are not wise and good, we have reason to wonder that there are any so. Were the Men as much neglected, and as little care taken to cultivate and improve them, perhaps they wou'd be so far from surpassing those whom they now despise, that they themselves wou'd sink into the greatest stupidity and brutality. The preposterous returns that the most of them make, to all the care and pains that is bestow'd on them, renders this no uncharitable, nor improbable Conjecture. One wou'd therefore almost think, that the wise disposer of all things, foreseeing how unjustly Women are denied opportunities of improvement from *without*, has therefore by way of compensation endow'd them with greater propensions to Vertue and a natural goodness of Temper *within*, which if duly manag'd would raise them to the most eminent pitch of heroick Vertue. Hither, Ladies, I desire you wou'd aspire, 'tis a noble and becoming Ambition, and to remove such Obstacles as lie in your way is the design of this Paper. We will therefore enquire what it is that stops your flight, that keeps you groveling here below, like *Domitian* catching Flies when you should be busied in obtaining Empires.

Altho' it has been said by Men of more Wit than Wisdom, and perhaps of more malice than either, that Women are naturally incapable of acting Prudently, or that they are necessarily determined to folly, I must by no meanes grant it; that Hypothesis would render my endeavours impertinent, for then it would be in vain to advise the one, or endeavour the Reformation of the other. Besides, there are Examples in all Ages, which sufficiently confute the Ignorance and Malice of this Assertion.

The Incapacity, if there be any, is acquired not natural, and none of their Follies are so necessary, but that they might avoid them if they pleas'd themselves. Some disadvantages indeed they labour under, and what these are we shall see by and by and endeavour to surmount; but Women need not take up with mean things, since (if they are not wanting to themselves) they are capable of the best. Neither God nor Nature have excluded them from being Ornaments to their Families and useful in their Generation; there is therefore no reason they should be content to be Cyphers in the World, useless at the best, and in a little time a burden and nuisance to all about them. And 'tis very great pity that they who are so apt to overrate themselves in smaller Matters, shou'd, where it most concerns them to know and stand upon their Value, be so insensible of their own worth. The Cause therefore of the defects we labour under is, if not wholly, yet at least in the first place, to be ascribed to the mistakes of our Education, which like an Error in the first Concoction, spreads its ill Influence through all our Lives.

The Soil is rich and would if well cultivated produce a noble Harvest, if then the Unskilful Managers, not only permit, but incourage noxious Weeds, tho' we shall suffer by the Neglect, yet they ought not in justice to blame any but themselves, if they reap the Fruit of this their foolish Conduct. Women are from their very Infancy debar'd those Advantages, with the want of which they are afterwards reproached, and nursed up in those Vices which will hereafter be upbraided to them. So partial are Men as to expect Brick where they afford no Straw; and so abundantly civil as to take care we shou'd make good that obliging Epithet of *Ignorant*, which out of an excess of good Manners, they are pleas'd to bestow on us!

One would be apt to think indeed, that Parents shou'd take all possible care of their Childrens Education, not only for *their* sakes, but even for their *own*. And tho' the Son convey the Name to Posterity, yet certainly a great Part of the Honour of their Families depends on their Daughters. 'Tis the kindness of Education that binds our duty fastest on us: For the being instrumental to the bringing of us into the world, is no matter of choice and therefore the less obliging; But to procure that we may live wisely and happily in it, and be capable of endless Joys hereafter, is a benefit we can never sufficiently acknowledge. To introduce poor Children into the World and neglect to fence them against the temptations of it, and so leave them expos'd to temporal and eternal Miseries, is a wickedness for which I want a Name; 'tis beneath Brutality; the Beasts are better natur'd, for they take care of their off-spring, till they are capable of caring for themselves. And if Mothers had a due regard to their Posterity, how *Great* soever they are, they would not think themselves too *Good* to perform what Nature requires, nor through Pride and Delicacy remit the poor little one to the care of a Foster Parent. Or if necessity inforce them to depute another to perform *their* Duty, they wou'd be as choice at least, in the Manners and Inclinations, as they are in the complections of their Nurses, lest with their Milk they transfuse their Vices, and form in the Child such evil habits as will not easily be eradicated.

Nature as bad as it is and as much as it is complain'd of, is so far improveable by the grace of GOD, upon our honest and hearty endeavours, that if we are not wanting to our selves, we may all in *some*, tho' not in an *equal* measure, be instruments of his Glory, Blessings to this World, and capable of Eternal Blessedness in that to come. But if our Nature is spoil'd, instead of being improv'd, at first; if from our Infancy we are nursed up in Ignorance and Vanity; are taught to be Proud and Petulant, Delicate and Fantastick, Humorous and Inconstant, 'tis not strange that the ill effects of this Conduct appear in all the future Actions of our Lives. And seeing it is Ignorance, either habitual or actual, which is the cause of all sin, how are they like to escape *this*, who are bred up in *that?* That therefore Women are unprofitable to most, and a plague and dishonour to some Men is not much to be regretted on account of the *Men*, because 'tis the product of their own folly, in denying them the benefits of an ingenuous and liberal Education, the most effectual means to direct them into, and to secure their progress in the ways of Vertue.

For that Ignorance is the cause of most Feminine Vices, may be instanc'd in that Pride and Vanity which is usually imputed to us, and which I suppose if throughly sifted, will appear to be some way or other, the rise and Original of all the rest. These, tho' very bad Weeds, are the product of a good Soil, they are nothing else but Generosity degenerated and corrupted. A desire to advance and perfect its Being, is planted by GOD in all

7

Rational Natures, to excite them hereby to every worthy and becoming Action; for certainly next to the Grace of GOD, nothing does so powerfully restrain people from Evil and stir them up to Good, as a generous Temper. And therefore to be ambitious of perfections is no fault, tho' to assume the Glory of our Excellencys to our selves, or to Glory in such as we really have not, are. And were Womens haughtiness express'd in disdaining to do a mean and evil thing, wou'd they pride themselves in somewhat truly perfective of a Rational nature, there were no hurt in it. But then they ought not to be denied the means of examining and judging what is so; they should not be impos'd on with tinsel ware. If by reason of a false Light, or undue Medium, they chuse amiss, theirs is the loss, but the Crime is the Deceivers. She who rightly understands wherein the perfection of her Nature consists, will lay out her Thoughts and Industry in the acquisition of such Perfections: But she who is kept ignorant of the matter, will take up with such Objects as first offer themselves, and bear any plausible resemblance to what she desires; a shew of advantage being sufficient to render them agreeable baits to her who wants Judgment and Skill to discern between reality and pretence. From whence it easily follows, that she who has nothing else to value her self upon, will be proud of her Beauty, or Mony and what that can purchase, and think her self mightily oblig'd to him, who tells her she has those Perfections which she naturally longs for. Her inbred self esteem and desire of good, which are degenerated into Pride and mistaken Self-love, will easily open her Ears to whatever goes about to nourish and delight them; and when a cunning designed Enemy from without, has drawn over to his Party these Traitors within, he has the Poor unhappy Person at his Mercy, who now very glibly swallows down his Poison, because 'tis presented in a Golden Cup, and credulously hearkens to the most disadvantageous Proposals, because they come attended with a seeming esteem. She whose Vanity makes her swallow praises by the whole sale, without examining whether she deserves them, or from what hand they come, will reckon it but gratitude to think well of him who values her so much, and think she must needs be merciful to the poor despairing Lover whom her Charms have reduc'd to die at her feet. Love and Honour are what every one of us naturally esteem, they are

8

excellent things in themselves and very worthy our regard, and by how much the readier we are to embrace whatever resembles them, by so much the more dangerous it is that these venerable Names should be wretchedly abus'd and affixt to their direct contraries, yet this is the Custom of the World: And how can she possibly detect the fallacy, who has no better Notion of either than what she derives from Plays and Romances? How can she be furnished with any solid Principles whose very Instructors are Froth and emptiness? Whereas Women were they rightly Educated, had they obtain'd a well inform'd and discerning Mind, they would be proof against all those Batteries, see through and scorn those little silly Artifices which are us'd to ensnare and deceive them. Such an one would value her self only on her Vertue, and consequently be most chary of what she esteems so much. She would know, that not what others *say*, but what she her self *does*, is the true Commendation and the only thing that exalts her; the loudest Encomiums being not half so satisfactory, as the calm and secret Plaudit of her own Mind, which moving on true Principles of Honour and Vertue, wou'd not fail on a review of it self to anticipate that delightful Eulogy she shall one day hear.

Whence is it but from ignorance, from a want of Understanding to compare and judge of things, to chuse a right End, to proportion the Means to the End, and to rate ev'ry thing according to its proper value, that we quit the Substance for the Shadow, Reality for Appearance, and embrace those very things which if we understood we shou'd hate and fly, but now are reconcil'd to, merely because they usurp the Name, tho' they have nothing of the Nature of those venerable Objects we desire and seek? Were it not for this delusion, is it probable a Lady who passionately desires to be admir'd, shou'd ever consent to such Actions as render her base and contemptible? Wou'd she be so absurd as to think either to get love, or to keep it, by those methods which occasion loathing and consequently end in hatred? Wou'd she reckon it a piece of her Grandeur, or hope to gain esteem by such excesses as really lessen her in the eyes of all considerate and judicious persons? Wou'd she be so silly as to look big and think her self the better person because she has more Money to bestow profusely, or the good luck to have a more ingenious Taylor or Milliner than her Neighbour? Wou'd she, who by the regard she pays to Wit, seems to make some pretences to it, undervalue her Judgment so much as to admit the Scurrility and profane noisy Nonsense of men, whose Fore heads are better than their Brains, to pass under that Character? Wou'd she be so weak as to imagine that a few airy Fancies joyn'd with a great deal of Impudence and Ill-nature (the right definition of modern Wit) can bespeak him a Man of sense, who runs counter to all the sense and reason that ever appear'd in the World? than which nothing can be an Argument of greater shallowness, unless it be to regard and esteem him for it. Wou'd a Woman, if she truly understood her self, be affected either with the praises or calumnies of those worthless persons, whose Lives are a direct contradiction to Reason, a very sink of corruption, by whom one wou'd blush to be commended, lest they shou'd be mistaken for Partners in or Connivers at their Crimes? Will she who has a jot of discernment think to satisfy her greedy desire of Pleasure, with those promising nothings that have again and again deluded her? Or will she to obtain such Bubbles, run the risque of forfeiting Joys infinitely satisfying and eternal? In sum, did not ignorance impose on us, we would never lavish out the greatest part of our Time and Care, on the decoration of a Tenement, in which our Lease is so very short, and which for all our industry, may loose it's Beauty e'er that Lease be out, and in the mean while neglect a more glorious and durable Mansion! We wou'd never be so curious of the House and so careless of the Inhabitant, whose beauty is capable of great improvement and will endure for ever without diminution or decay!

Thus Ignorance and a narrow Education lay the Foundation of Vice, and Imitation and Custom rear it up. Custom, that merciless torrent that carries all before it, and which indeed can be stem'd by none but such as have a great deal of Prudence and a rooted Virtue. For 'tis but Decorous that she who is not capable of giving better Rules, shou'd follow those she sees before her, least she only change the instance and retain the absurdity. 'Twou'd puzzle a considerate Person to account for all that Sin and Folly that is in the World (which certainly has nothing in it self to recommend it) did not Custom help to solve the difficulty. For Virtue without question has on all accounts the preeminence of Vice, 'tis abundantly more pleasant in the *Act*, as well as more advantageous in the *Consequences*, as any one who will but rightly use her reason, in a serious reflection on her self and the nature of things, may easily perceive. 'Tis Custom, therefore, that Tyrant Custom, which is the grand motive to all those irrational choices which we daily see made in the World, so very contrary to our *present* interest and pleasure, as well as to our Future. We think it an unpardonable mistake not to do as our neighbours do, and part with our Peace and Pleasure as well as our Innocence and Virtue, meerly in complyance with an unreasonable Fashion, and having inur'd our selves to Folly, we know not how to quit it; we go on in Vice, not because we find satisfaction in it, but because we are unacquainted with the Joys of Virtue.

Add to this the hurry and noise of the World, which does generally so busy and pre-ingage us, that we have little time and less inclination to stand still and reflect on our own Minds. Those impertinent Amusements which have seiz'd us, keep their hold so well and so constantly buz about our Ears, that we cannot atten l to the Dictates of our Reason, nor to the soft whispers and winning persuasives of the divine Spirit, by whose assistance were we dispos'd to make use of it, we might shake off these Follies and regain our Freedom. But alas! to complete our misfortunes, by a continual application to Vanity and Folly, we quite spoil the contexture and frame of our Minds, so loosen and dissipate, that nothing solid and substantial will stay in them. By an habitual inadvertency we render our selves incapable of any serious and improving thought, till our minds themselves become as light and frothy as those things they are conversant about. To all which if we further add the great industry that bad people use to corrupt the good, and that unaccountable backwardness that appears in too many good persons, to stand up for and propagate the Piety they profess; (so strangely are things transposed, that Vertue puts on the blushes which belong to Vice, and Vice insults with the authority of Virtue!) and we have a pretty fair account of the Causes of our non-improvement.

When a poor Young Lady is taught to value her self on nothing but her Cloaths, and to think she's very fine when well accoutred; When she hears say, that 'tis Wisdom enough for her to know how to dress her self, that she may become amiable in his eyes, to whom it appertains to be knowing and learned;

who can blame her if she lay out her Industry and Money on such Accomplishments, and sometimes extends it farther than her misinformer desires she should? When she sees the vain and the gay, making *Parade* in the World and attended with the Courtship and admiration of the gazing herd, no wonder that her tender Eyes are dazled with the Pageantry, and wanting Judgment to pass a due Estimate on them and their Admirers, longs to be such a fine and celebrated thing as they? What tho' she be sometimes told of another World, she has however a more lively perception of this, and may well think, that if her Instructors were in earnest when they tell her of *hereafter*, they would not be so busied and concerned about what happens *here*. She is it may be, taught the Principles and Duties of Religion, but not Acquainted with the Reasons and Grounds of them; being told 'tis enough for her to believe, to examine why, and wherefore, belongs not to her. And therefore, though her Piety may be tall and spreading, yet because it wants Foundation and Root, the first rude Temptation overthrows and blasts it, or perhaps the short liv'd Gourd decays and withers of its own accord. But why should she be blamed for setting no great value on her Soul, whose noblest Faculty her Understanding is render'd useless to her? Or censur'd for relinquishing a course of Life, whose Prerogatives she was never acquainted with, and tho highly reasonable in it self, was put upon the embracing it with as little reason as she now forsakes it? For if her Religion it self be taken up as the Mode of the Country, 'tis no strange thing that she lays it down again in conformity to the Fashion. Whereas she whose Reason is suffer'd to display it self, to inquire into the grounds and Motives of Religion, to make a disquisition of its Graces and search out its hidden Beauties; who is a Christian out of Choice, not in conformity to those among whom she lives; and cleaves to Piety, because 'tis her Wisdom, her Interest, her Joy, not because she has been accustom'd to it; she who is not only eminently and unmovably good, but able to give a Reason *why* she is so, is too firm and stable to be mov'd by the pitiful Allurements of sin, too wise and too well bottom'd to be undermin'd and supplanted by the strongest Efforts of Temptation. Doubtless a truly Christian Life requires a clear Understanding as well as regular Affections, that both together may move the Will to a direct choice of Good and a stedfast adherence to it. For tho' the heart may be honest, it is but by chance that the Will is right if the Understanding be Ignorant and Cloudy. And what's the reason that we sometimes see persons unhappily falling off from their Piety, but because 'twas their Affections, not their Judgment, that inclin'd them to be Religious? Reason and Truth are firm and immutable, she who bottoms on them is on sure ground, Humour and Inclination are sandy Foundations, and she who is sway'd by her Affections more than by her Judgment, owes the happiness of her Soul in a great measure to the temper of her Body; her Piety may perhaps blaze high but will not last long. For the Affections are various and changeable, mov'd by every Object, and the last comer easily undoes whatever its Predecessor had done before. Such Persons are always in extreams, they are either violently good or quite cold and indifferent; a perpetual trouble to themselves and others, by indecent Raptures, or unnecessary Scruples; there is no Beauty and order in their lives, all is rapid and unaccountable; they are now very furious in such a course, but they cannot well tell why, and anon as violent in the other extream. Having more *Heat* than *Light*, their Zeal outruns their Knowledge, and instead of representing Piety as it is in it self, the most lively and inviting thing imaginable, they expose it to the contempt and ridicule of the censorious World. Their devotion becomes ricketed, starv'd and contracted in some of it's vital parts, and disproportioned and over-grown in less material instances; whilst one Duty is *over-done* to commute for the neglect of another, and the mistaken person thinks the being often on her knees, attones for all the miscarriages of her Conversation: Not considering that 'tis in vain to petition for those Graces which we take no care to practise, and a mockery to adore those Perfections we run counter to, and that the true end of all our Prayers and external observances is to work our minds into a truly Christian temper, to obtain for us the Empire of our Passions, and to reduce all irregular Inclinations, that so we may be as like GOD in Purity, Charity, and all his imitable excellencies, as is consistent with the imperfection of a Creature.

And now having discovered the Disease and its cause, 'tis proper to apply a Remedy; single Medicines are too weak to cure such complicated Distempers, they require a full Dispensatory; and what wou'd a good Woman refuse to do, could she hope by that to advantage the greatest part of the World, and improve her Sex in Knowledge and true Religion? I doubt not, Ladies, but that the Age, as bad as it is, affords very many of you who will readily embrace whatever has a true tendency to the Glory of GOD and your mutual Edification, to revive the ancient Spirit of Piety in the World and to transmit it to succeeding Generations. I know there are many of you who so ardently love God, as to think no time too much to spend in his service, nor any thing too difficult to do for his sake; and bear such a hearty good will to your Neighbours, as to grudge no Prayers or Pains to reclaim and improve them. I have therefore no more to do but to make the Proposal, to prove that it will answer these great and good Ends, and then 'twill be easy to obviate the Objections that Persons of more Wit than Vertue may happen to raise against it.

Now as to the Proposal, it is to erect a *Monastery*, or if you will (to avoid giving offence to the scrupulous and injudicious, by names which tho' innocent in themselves, have been abus'd by superstitious Practices), we will call it a *Religious Retirement*, and such as shall have a double aspect, being not only a Retreat from the World for those who desire that advantage, but likewise, an Institution and previous discipline, to fit us to do the greatest good in it; such an Institution as this (if I do not mightily receive my self) would be the most probable method to amend the present, and improve the future Age. For here those who are convinc'd of the emptiness of earthly Enjoyments, who are sick of the vanity of the world and its impertinencies, may find more substantial and satisfying entertainments, and need not be confin'd to what they justly loath. Those who are desirous to know and fortify their weak side, first do good to themselves, that hereafter they may be capable of doing more good to others; or for their greater security are willing to avoid *Temptation*, may get out of that danger which a continual stay in view of the Enemy, and the familiarity and unwearied application of the Temptation may expose them to; and gain an opportunity to look into themselves, to be acquainted at home and no longer the greatest strangers to their own hearts. Such as are willing in a more peculiar and undisturb'd manner, to attend the great business they came into the world about, the service of GOD and improvement of their own Minds, may find a convenient and blissful recess from the noise and hurry of the world. A world so cumbersom, so infectious, that altho' thro' the grace of GOD and their own strict watchfulness, they are kept from sinking down into its corruptions, 'twill however damp their flight to heav'n, hinder them from attaining any eminent pitch of Vertue.

You are therefore Ladies, invited into a place, where you shall suffer no other confinement, but to be kept out of the road of sin: You shall not be depriv'd of your Grandeur but only exchange the vain Pomps and Pageantry of the world, empty Titles and Forms of State, for the true and solid Greatness of being able to despise them. You will only quit the Chat of insignificant people for an ingenious Conversation; the froth of flashy Wit for real Wisdom; idle tales for instructive discourses. The deceitful Flatteries of those who under pretence of loving and admiring you, really served their *own* base ends, for the seasonable Reproofs and wholsom Counsels of your hearty well-wishers and affectionate Friends, which will procure you those perfections your feigned lovers pretended you had, and kept you from obtaining. No uneasy task will be enjoyn'd you, all your labour being only to prepare for the highest degrees of that Glory, the very lowest of which is more than at present you are able to conceive, and the prospect of it sufficient to outweigh all the Pains of Religion, were there any in it, as really there are none. All that is requir'd of you, is only to be as Happy as possibly you can, and to make sure of a Felicity that will fill all the capacities of your Souls! A happiness, which when once you have tasted, you'll be fully convinc'd you cou'd never do too much to obtain it, nor be too solicitous to adorn your Souls with such tempers and dispositions, as will at present make you in some measure, such holy and Heavenly Creatures as you one day hope to be in a more perfect manner; without which Qualifications you can neither reasonably *expect,* nor are *capable* of enjoying the Happiness of the Life to come. Happy Retreat! which will be the introducing you into such a *Paradise* as your Mother *Eve* forfeited, where you shall feast on Pleasures, that do not like those of the World, disappoint your expectations, pall your Appetites, and by the disgust they give you put you on the fruitless search after new Delights, which when obtain'd are as empty as the former; but such as will make you *truly* happy now, and prepare you to be *perfectly* so hereafter. Here are no Serpents to deceive you, whilst you entertain your selves in these delicious Gardens. No Provocations will be given in this Amicable Society, but to Love and to good Works, which will afford such an entertaining employment, that you'll have as little inclination as leisure to pursue those Follies, which in the time of your ignorance pass'd with you under the name of love, altho' there is not in nature two more different things, than *true Love* and that *brutish Passion*, which pretends to ape it. Here will be no Rivalling but for the Love of GOD, no Ambition but to procure his Favour, to which nothing will more effectually recommend you, than a great and dear affection to each other. Envy that Canker, will not here disturb your Breasts; for how can she repine at anothers well-fare, who reckons it the greatest part of her own? No Covetousness will gain admittance in this blest abode, but to amass huge Treasures of good Works, and to procure one of the brightest Crowns of Glory. You will not be solicitous to encrease your Fortunes, but to enlarge your Minds, esteeming no Grandeur like being conformable to the meek and humble JESUS. So that you only withdraw from the noise and trouble, the folly and temptation of the world, that you may more peaceably enjoy your selves, and all the innocent Pleasures it is able to afford you, and particularly that which is worth all the rest, a noble, Vertuous and Disinterest'd Friendship. And to compleat all, that *Acme* of delight which the devout Seraphic Soul enjoys when dead to the World, she devotes her self entirely to the Contemplation and Fruition of her Beloved; when having disengag'd her self from all those Lets which hindred her from without, she moves in a direct and vigorous motion towards her true and only Good, whom now she embraces and acquiesces in with such an unspeakable pleasure, as is only intelligible to those who have tried and felt it, which we can no more describe to the dark and sensual part of Mankind, than we can the beauty of Colours and harmony of Sounds to the Blind and Deaf. In fine, the place to which you are invited is a Type and Antepast of Heav'n, where your Employments will be as there, to magnify GOD, to love one another, and to communicate that useful Knowledge, which by the due improvement of your time in Study and Contemplation you will obtain, and which when obtain'd will afford you a much sweeter and more durable delight, than all those pitiful diversions, those revellings and amusements, which now thro' your ignorance of better, appear the only grateful and relishing Entertainments.

But because we were not made for our selves, nor can by any means so effectually glorify GOD, and do good to our own Souls, as by doing Offices of Charity and Beneficence to others; and to the intent that every Vertue, and the highest degrees of every Vertue may be exercis'd and promoted the most that may be; your Retreat shall be so manag'd as not to exclude the good Works of an *Active*, from the pleasure and serenity of a *Contemplative* Life, but by a due mixture of both retain all the advantages and avoid the inconveniencies that attend either. It shall not so cut you off from the world as to hinder you from bettering and improving it, but rather qualify you to do it the greatest Good, and be a Seminary to stock the Kingdom with pious and prudent Ladies, whose good Example it is to be hop'd, will so influence the rest of their Sex, that Women may no longer pass for those little useless and impertinent Animals, which the ill conduct of too many has caus'd 'em to be mistaken for.

We have hitherto consider'd our Retirement only in relation to Religion, which is indeed its *main*, I may say its *only* design; nor can this be thought too contracting a word, since Religion is the adequate business of our lives, and largely consider'd, takes in all we have to do, nothing being a fit employment for a rational Creature, which has not either a *direct* or *remote* tendency to this great and *only* end. But because, as we have all along observ'd, Religion never appears in it's true Beauty, but when it is accompanied with Wisdom and Discretion; and that without a good Understanding, we can scarce be *truly*, but never *eminently* Good; being liable to a thousand seductions and mistakes (for even the men themselves, if they have not a competent degree of Knowledge, are carried about with every wind of Doctrine). Therefore, one great end of this Institution shall be, to expel that cloud of Ignorance which Custom has involv'd us in, to furnish our minds with a stock of solid and useful Knowledge, that the Souls of Women may no longer be the only unadorn'd and neglected things. It is not intended that our *Religious* shou'd waste their time, and trouble their heads about such unconcerning matters, as the vogue of the world has turn'd up for Learning, the impertinency of which

Mr. Nor.
Conduct
of Hum.
Life.

has been excellently expos'd by an ingenious Pen, but busy themselves in a serious enquiry after *necessary* and *perfective* truths, something which it *concerns* them to know, and which tends to their real interest and perfection, and what that is the excellent Author just now mention'd will sufficiently inform them. Such a course of Study will neither be too troublesome nor out of the reach of a Female Virtuoso; for it is not intended she shou'd spend her hours in learning *words* but *things*, and therefore no more Languages than are necessary to acquaint her with useful Authors. Nor need she trouble her self in turning over a great number of Books, but take care to understand and digest a few well chosen and good ones. Let her but obtain right Ideas, and be truly acquainted with the nature of those Objects that present themselves to her mind, and then no matter whether or no she be able to tell what fanciful people have said about them: And thoroughly to understand Christianity as profess'd by the *Church* of *England,* will be sufficient to confirm her in the truth, tho' she have not a Catalogue of those particular errors which oppose it. Indeed a Learned Education of the Women will appear so unfashionable, that I began to startle at the singularity of the proposition, but was extremely pleas'd

Mr.
Wotton's
Reflects.
on Ant.
and Mod.
Lear, p.
349, 350.

when I found a late ingenious Author (whose Book I met with since the writing of this) agree with me in my Opinion. For speaking of the Repute that Learning was in about 150 Years ago, *It was so very modish* (says he) *that the fair Sex seem'd to believe that* Greek *and* Latin *added to their Charms: and* Plato *and* Aristotle *untranslated, were frequent Ornaments of their Closets. One wou'd think by the effects, that it was a proper way of Educating them, since there are no accounts in History of so many great Women in any one Age, as are to be found between the years 15 and 1600.*

For since GOD has given Women as well as Men intelligent Souls, why should they be forbidden to improve them? Since he has not denied us the faculty of Thinking, why shou'd we not (at least in gratitude to him) employ our Thoughts on himself their noblest Object, and not unworthily bestow them on Trifles and Gaities and secular Affairs? Being the Soul was created for the contemplation of Truth as well as for the fruition

18

of Good, is it not as cruel and unjust to exclude Women from the knowledge of the one as from the enjoyment of the other? Especially since the Will is blind, and cannot chuse but by the direction of the Understanding; or to speak more properly, since the Soul always *Wills* according as she *Understands*, so that if she Understands amiss, she Wills amiss. And as Exercise enlarges and exalts any Faculty, so thro' want of using it becomes crampt and lessened; if therefore we make little or no use of our Understandings, we shall shortly have none to use; and the more contracted and unemploy'd the deliberating and directive Power is, the more liable is the elective to unworthy and mischievous choices. What is it but the want of an ingenious Education, that renders the generality of Feminine Conversations so insipid and foolish and their solitude so insupportable? Learning is therefore necessary to render them more agreeable and useful in company, and to furnish them with becoming entertainments when alone, that so they may not be driven to those miserable shifts, which too many make use of to put off their Time, that precious Talent that never lies on the hands of a judicious Person. And since our Happiness in the next World, depends so far on those dispositions which we carry along with us out of this, that without a right habitude and temper of mind we are not capable of Felicity; and seeing our Beatitude consists in the contemplation of the divine Truth and Beauty, as well as in the fruition of his Goodness, can Ignorance be a fit preparative for Heaven? Is't likely that she whose Understanding has been busied about nothing but froth and trifles, shou'd be capable of delighting her self in noble and sublime Truths? Let such therefore as deny us the improvement of our Intellectuals, either take up *his* Paradox, who said that *Women have no Souls*, which at a time when the most contend to have them allow'd to Brutes, wou'd be as unphilosophical as it is unmannerly, or else let them permit us to cultivate and improve them. There is a sort of Learning indeed which is worse than the greatest Ignorance: A Woman may study Plays and Romances all her days, and be a great deal more knowing but never a jot the wiser. Such a knowledge as this serves only to instruct and put her forward in the practice of the greatest Follies, yet how can they justly blame her who forbid, or at least won't afford opportunity of better? A rational mind *will* be employ'd, it will never be satisfy'd in doing nothing, and if you neglect to furnish it with good materials, 'tis like to take up with such as come to hand.

We pretend not that Women shou'd teach in the Church, or usurp Authority where it is not allow'd them; permit us only to understand our *own* duty, and not be forc'd to take it upon trust from others; to be at least so far learned, as to be able to form in our minds a true Idea of Christianity, it being so very necessary to fence us against the danger of these *last* and *perilous days,* in which Deceivers a part of whose Character is to *lead captive silly Women,* need not *creep into Houses* since they have Authority to proclaim their Errors on the *House top.* And let us also acquire a true Practical knowledge, such as will convince us of the absolute necessity of *Holy Living* as well as of *Right Believing,* and that no Heresy is more dangerous than that of an ungodly and wicked Life. And since the *French Tongue* is understood by most Ladies, methinks they may much better improve it by the study of Philosophy (as I hear the *French Ladies* do) *Des Cartes, Malebranche* and others, than by reading idle *Novels* and *Romances.* 'Tis strange we shou'd be so forward to imitate their Fashions and Fopperies, and have no regard to what really deserves our Imitation. And why shall it not be thought as genteel to understand *French Philosophy,* as to be accoutred in a *French Mode?* Let therefore the famous Madam *D'acier, Scudery,* &c, and our own incomparable *Orinda,* excite the Emulation of the English Ladies.

The Ladies, I'm sure, have no reason to dislike this Proposal, but I know not how the Men will resent it to have their enclosure broke down, and Women invited to taste of that Tree of knowledge they have so long unjustly *Monopoliz'd.* But they must excuse me, if I be as partial to my own Sex as they are to theirs, and think Women as capable of Learning as Men are, and that it becomes them as well. For I cannot imagine wherein the hurt lies, if instead of doing mischief to one another, by an uncharitable and vain Conversation, Women be enabled to inform and instruct those of their own Sex at least; the Holy Ghost having left it on record, that *Priscilla* as well as her Husband, catechiz'd the eloquent *Apollos* and the great Apostle found no fault with her. It will therefore be very proper for our Ladies to spend part of their time in this Retirement, in adorning their minds with useful Knowledge.

To enter into the detail of the particulars concerning the Government of the *Religious*, their Offices of Devotion, Employments, Work &c. is not now necessary. Suffice it at present to signify, that they will be more than ordinarily careful to redeem their Time, spending no more of it on the Body than the necessities of Nature require, but by a judicious choice of their Employment and a constant industry about it, so improve this invaluable Treasure, that it may neither be buried in Idleness, nor lavish'd out in unprofitable concerns. For a stated portion of it being daily paid to GOD in Prayers and Praises, the rest shall be imploy'd in innocent, charitable, and useful Business; either in study in learning themselves or instructing others, for it is design'd that part of their Employment be the Education of those of their own Sex; or else in spiritual and corporal Works of Mercy, relieving the Poor, healing the Sick, mingling Charity to the Soul with that they express to the Body, instructing the Ignorant, counselling the Doubtful, comforting the Afflicted, and correcting those that err and do amiss.

And as it will be the business of their lives, their meat and drink to *know* and *do* the Will of their Heavenly Father, so will they pay a strict conformity to all the Precepts of their holy Mother the *Church*, whose sacred Injunctions are too much neglected, even by those who pretend the greatest zeal for her. For besides the daily performance of the Publick Offices after the Cathedral manner, in the most affecting and elevating way, the celebration of the Holy Eucharist every Lords Day and Holy-day, and a course of solid instructive Preaching and Catechizing; our *Religious*, considering that the Holy JESUS punctually observ'd the innocent usages of the *Jewish* Church, and tho' in many instances the *Reason* of the Command ceas'd as to him, yet he wou'd obey the *letter* to avoid giving offence and to set us an admirable pattern of Obedience; therefore, tho' it may be thought such pious Souls have little occasion for the severities of fasting and mortification, yet they will consider it as a special part of their Duty to observe all the Fasts of the Church, *viz. Lent, Ember*, and *Rogation-days, Fridays*, and *Vigils;* times so little heeded by the most, that one wou'd scarce believe them set apart for Religious Purposes, did we not find them in the antiquated Rubricks. And as their Devotion will be regular, so shall it likewise be solid and substantial. They will not rest in the mere out-side of Duty, nor fansie the performance of their Fasts and Offices will procure them license to indulge a darling Vice: But having long since laid the Ax to the root of sin, and destroy'd the whole body of it, they will look upon these holy times of recollection and extraordinary Devotion (without which Fasting signifies little) as excellent means to keep it down, and to pluck up every the least Fibre that may happen to remain in them. But we intend not by this to impose any intolerable burden on tender Constitutions, knowing that our Lord has taught us, that Mercy is to be preferr'd before Sacrifice: and that Bodily Exercise profiteth but a little, the chief business being to obtain a divine and God-like temper of Mind.

And as this institution will strictly enjoyn all pious and profitable Employments, so does it not only permit but recommend harmless and ingenious Diversions, Musick particularly, and such as may refresh the Body without enervating the Mind. They do a disservice to Religion who make it an enemy to innocent Nature, and injure the Almighty when they represent him as imposing burdens that are not to be born. Neither GOD nor Wise men will like us the better for an affected severity and waspish sourness. Nature and Grace will never disagree, provided we mistake not the one, nor indulge the petulancy of the other; there being no Displacencies in Religion, but what we our selves have unhappily made. For true Piety is the most sweet and engaging thing imaginable, as it is most obliging to others, so most easie to our selves. 'Tis in truth the highest *Epicurism*, exalting our Pleasures by refining them; keeping our Appetites in that due regularity which not only Grace, but even Nature and Reason require, in the breach of which tho' there may be a Transport, there can be no true and substantial delight.

As to *Lodging, Habit* and *Diet*, they may be quickly resolv'd on by the Ladies who shall subscribe; who I doubt not will make choice of what is most plain and decent, what Nature not Luxury requires. And since neither Meat nor Cloaths commend us unto GOD, they'll content themselves with such things as are fit and convenient, without occasioning scruple to themselves or giving any trouble or offence to others. She who considers to how much better account that Money will turn which is bestow'd on the Poor, than that which is laid out in unnecessary Expences on her self, needs no Admonitions against superfluities. She who truly loves her self, will never waste that Money on a decaying Carkass, which if prudently disburs'd wou'd procure her an eternal Mansion. She will never think her self so fine, as when the backs of the Poor do bless her; and never feast so luxuriously as when she treats an hungry person. No perfume will be thought so grateful as the Odour of Good Works, nor any Wash so Beautifying as her own tears. For her Heroick Soul is too great to ambition any Empire but that of her own Breast, or to regard any other Conquest than the rescuing poor unhappy Souls from the slavery of Sin and Satan, those only unsupportable Tyrants; and therefore what Decays she observes in her face will be very unconcerning, but she will with greatest speed and accuracy rectify the least Spot that may prejudice the beauty of her lovely Soul.

In a word, this happy Society will be but one Body, whose Soul is love—animating and informing us; and perpetually breathing forth it self in flames of holy desires after GOD and acts of Benevolence to each other. Envy and Uncharitableness are the Vices only of little and narrow hearts, and therefore 'tis suppos'd, they will not enter here amongst persons whose Dispositions as well as their Births are to be Generous. Censure will refine into Friendly Admonition, all Scoffing and offensive Railleries will be abominated and banish'd hence, where not only the Words and Actions, but even the very Thoughts and Desires of the *Religious* tend to promote the most endearing Love and universal Good-will. Thus these innocent and holy Souls shou'd run their Race, measuring their hours by their Devotions, and their days by the charitable Works they do. Thus wou'd they live the life of Heaven whilst on Earth, and receive an Earnest of its Joys in their hearts. And now, what remains for them to do at Night, but to review the Actions of the Day? to examine what Passions have been stirring? How their Devotions were performed? in what temper their Hearts are? what good they have done? what progress they've made towards Heaven? and with the plaudit of a satisfied Conscience sweetly to sleep in peace and safety, Angels pitching their Tents round about them, and he that neither slumbers nor sleeps rejoycing over them to do them good.

And to the end that these great designs may be the better pursu'd and effectually obtain'd, care shall be taken that our *Religious* be under the tuition of persons of irreproachable Lives, of a consummate Prudence, sincere Piety and unaffected Gravity. No Novices in Religion, but such as have spent the greatest part of their lives in the study and practice of Christianity; who have lived *much*, whatever the time of their abode in the world has been. Whose Understandings are clear and comprehensive, as well as their Passions at command and Affections regular, and their Knowledge able to govern their Zeal. Whose scrutiny into their own hearts has been so exact, that they fully understand the weaknesses of humane Nature, are able to bear with its defects, and by the most prudent methods procure its Amendment. Plentifully furnish'd with instructions for the Ignorant and comfort for the disconsolate; who know how to quicken the slothful, to awaken the secure, and to dispel the doubts of the Scrupulous. Who are not ignorant when to use the Spur and when the Rein, but duly qualified to minister to all the spiritual wants of their Charge; Watching over their Souls with tenderness and prudence; applying fitting Medicines with sweetness and affability. Sagacious in discovering the very approaches of a fault, wise in preventing, and charitable in bearing with all pityable Infirmities. The sweetness of whose Nature is commensurate to all the rest of their good Qualities, and all conspire together to make them lov'd and reverenc'd. Who have the perfect government of themselves, and therefore rule according to Reason not Humour, consulting the good of the Society, not their own arbitrary sway. Yet know how to assert their Authority when there is just occasion for it, and will not prejudice their Charge by an indiscreet remissness and loosning the Reins of discipline. But what occasion will there be for rigour, when the design is to represent Vertue in all her Charms and native Loveliness, which must needs attract the eyes and enamour the hearts of all who behold her? To joyn the sweetness of Humanity to the strictness of Philosophy, that both together being improv'd and heighten'd by grace, may make up an accomplish'd *Christian*, for she who is truly so, is certainly the best-bred and best natur'd person in the world, adorn'd with a thousand Charms, most happy in her self and most agreeable and beneficial to all She converses with? And that every one who comes under this holy Roof may be such an amiable, such a charming Creature, what faults they bring with them shall be corrected by sweetness not severity; by friendly Admonitions, not magisterial Reproofs;

Piety shall not be roughly impos'd but wisely insinuated, by a perpetual Display of the Beauties of Religion in an exemplary Conversation, the continual and most powerful Sermon of an holy life. And since Inclination can't be forc'd, and nothing makes people more uneasy than the fettering themselves with unnecessary Bonds, there shall be no Vows or irrevocable Obligations, not so much as the fear of Reproach to keep our Ladies here any longer than they desire. No: Ev'ry act of our *Religious* Votary shall be voluntary and free, and no other tye but the Pleasure, the Glory and Advantage of this blessed retirement to confine her to it.

And now I suppose, you'll save me the labour of proving, that this Institution will very much serve the ends of Piety and Charity; it is methinks self-evident, and the very Proposal sufficient proof. But if it will not promote these great ends, I shall think my self mightily oblig'd to him who will shew me what will; for provided the good of my Neighbour be advanc'd, 'tis very indifferent to me whether it be my method or by anothers. Here will be no impertinent Visits, no foolish Amours, no idle Amusements to distract our Thoughts and waste our precious time; a very little of which is spent in Dressing, that grand devourer and its concomitants, and no more than necessity requires in sleep and eating; so that here's a vast Treasure gain'd, which for ought I know may purchase an happy Eternity. But we need not rest in generals, a cursory view of some particulars will sufficiently demonstrate the great usefulness of such a Retirement; which will appear by observing first a few of those inconveniencies to which Ladies are expos'd by living in the World, and in the next place the positive advantages of a Retreat.

And first, as to the inconveniencies of living in the World; no very small one is that strong *Idea* and warm perception it gives us of its Vanities; since these are ever at hand, constantly thronging about us, they must necessarily push aside all other Objects, and the Mind being prepossess'd and gratefully entertain'd with those pleasing Perceptions which external Objects occasion, takes up with them as its only Good, is not at leisure to taste those delights which arise from a Reflection on it self, nor to receive the *Ideas* which such a Reflection conveys, and consequently forms all its Notions by such *Ideas* only as it derives from sensation, being unacquainted with those more excellent ones which arise from its own operations and a serious reflection on them, and which are necessary to correct the mistakes and supply the defects of the other. From whence arises a very partial knowledge of things, nay, almost a perfect ignorance in things of the greatest moment. For tho' we are acquainted with the Sound of some certain words, *viz. God, Religion, Pleasure* and *Pain, Honour* and *Dishonour,* and the like; yet having no other *Ideas* but what are convey'd to us by those Trifles we converse with, we frame to our selves strange and awkward notions of them, conformable only to those *Ideas* sensation has furnish'd us with, which sometimes grow so strong and fixt, that 'tis scarce possible to introduce a new Scheme of Thoughts and so to disabuse us, especially whilst these Objects are thick in our way.

Thus she who sees her self and others respected in proportion to that Pomp and Bustle they make in the world, will form her Idea of Honour accordingly. She who has relish'd no Pleasures but such as arise at the presence of outward Objects, will seek no higher than her Senses for her Gratification. And thus we may account for that strange insensibility, that appears in some people when you speak to them of any serious Religious matter. They are then so dull you'll have much ado to make them understand the clearest Truth: Whereas if you rally the same persons, or chat with them of some Mode or Foppery, they'll appear very quick, expert, and ingenious. I have sometimes smil'd betwixt scorn and pity, to hear Women talk as gravely and concernedly about some trifling disappointment from their Millener or Taylor, as if it had related to the weightiest concerns of their Souls, nay, perhaps more seriously than others who wou'd pass for Good, do about their eternal Interest; but turn the talk that way, and they grow as heavy and cold as they were warm and sensible before. And whence is this, but because their heads are full of the one, and quite destitute of such Ideas as might give them a competent notion of the other, and therefore to discourse of such matters, is as little to the purpose as to make Mathematical Demonstrations to one who knows not what an Angle or Triangle means. Hence by the way, will appear the great usefulness of judicious Catechizing, which is necessary to form clear Ideas in the mind, without which it can receive but little benefit from the Discourses of the Pulpit, and perhaps the neglect of the former, is the reason that the great plenty of the latter has no better effect. By all which it appears, that if we wou'd not be impos'd on by false Representations and Impostures, if we wou'd obtain a due knowledge, of the most important things, we must remove the little Toys and Vanities of the world from us, or our selves from them; enlarge our Ideas, seek out new Fields of knowledge, whereby to rectify our first mistakes.

From the same Original, *viz.* the constant flattery of external Objects, arises that querulousness and delicacy observable in most Persons of fortune, and which betrays them to many inconveniencies. For besides that it renders them altogether unfit to bear a change, which considering the great uncertainty and swift vicissitudes of worldly things, the Greatest and most established ought not to be unprepar'd for; it likewise makes them perpetually uneasy, abates the delight of their enjoyments, for such persons will very rarely find all things to their mind, and then some little disorder which others wou'd take no notice of, like an aching Tooth or Toe, spoils the relish of their Joys. And tho' many great Ladies affect this temper, mistaking it for a piece of Grandeur, 'tis so far from that, that it gives evidence of a poor weak Mind, a very childish Humour, that must be cocker'd and fed with Toys and Baubles to still its frowardness, and is like the crazy stomach of a sick Person, which no body has reason to be fond of or desire.

This also disposes them to Inconstancy, for she who is continually supply'd with variety knows not where to fix; a Vice which some Women seem to be proud of, and yet nothing in the World so reproachful and degrading, because nothing is a stronger indication of a weak and injudicious mind. For it supposes us either so ignorant as to make a wrong Choice at first, or else so silly as not to know and stick to it, when we have made a right one. It bespeaks an unthinking inconsiderate Mind, one that lives at Random, without any design or end; who wanting judgment to discern where to fix, or to know when she's well, is ever fluctuating and uncertain, undoing to day what she had done yesterday, which is the worst Character that can be given of ones Understanding.

A constant Scene of Temptations and the infection of ill company, is another danger which conversing in the world exposes to. 'Tis a dangerous thing to have all the opportunities of sinning in our power, and the danger is increas'd by the ill Precedents we daily see of those who take them. *Liberty* (as some body says) *will corrupt an Angel,* and tho' it is indeed more glorious to conquer than to fly, yet since our Vertue is so visibly weakned in other instances, we have no reason to presume on't in this. 'Tis become no easy matter to secure our Innocence in our necessary Civilities and daily Conversations, in which if we have the good luck to avoid such as bring a necessity on us, either of seeming rude to them, or of being really so to GOD Almighty, whilst we tamely hear him, our best Friend and Bene-factor affronted, and swallow it, at the same time, that we wou'd reckon't a very pitiful Spirit to hear an Acquaintance traduc'd and hold our Tongue; yet if we avoid this Trial, our Charity is however in continual danger, Censoriousness being grown so modish, that we can scarce avoid being active or passive in it; so that she who has not her pert jest ready to pass upon others, shall as soon as her back is turn'd, become a Jest her self for want of Wit.

In consequence of all this, we are insensibly betray'd to a great loss of time, a Treaure whose value we are too often quite ignorant of till it be lost past redemption. And yet considering the shortness and uncertainty of Life, the great work we have to do, and what advantages accrue to us by a due management of our time, we cannot reconcile it with prudence to suffer the least minute to escape us. But besides our own lavish Expences concerning which one may ask as *Solomon* does of Labour, *What Fruit have we of all that Sport and Pastime we have taken under the Sun?* so unreasonable is the humour of the World, that those who wou'd reckon it a rudeness to make so bold with our Money, never scruple to waste and rob us of this infinitely more precious Treasure.

In the last place, by reason of this loss of time and the con-tinual hurry we are in, we can find no opportunities for thought-fulness and recollection; we are so busied with what passes abroad, that we have no leisure to look at home, nor to rectifie the disorders there. And such an unthinking mechanical way of living, when like Machines we are condemn'd every day to repeat the impertinencies of the day before, shortens our Views, con-tracts our Minds, exposes to a thousand practical Errors, and renders Improvement impossible, because it will not permit us to consider and recollect, which is the only means to attain it. So much for the inconveniences of living in the World; if we enquire concerning Retirement, we shall find it does not only remove all these, but brings considerable advantages of its own.

For first, it helps us to mate Custom and delivers us from its Tyranny, which is the most considerable thing we have to do, it being nothing else but the habituating our selves to Folly that can reconcile us to it. But how hard is is to quit an old road? What courage as well as prudence does it require? How clear a Judgment to overlook the Prejudices of Education and Example, and to discern what is best, and how strong a Resolution, notwithstanding all the Scoffs and Noises of the world, to adhere to it? For Custom has usurpt such an unaccountable Authority, that she would endeavour to put a stop to its Arbitrary Sway and reduce it to Reason, is in a fair way to render herself the *Butt* for all the Fops in Town to shoot their impertinent Censures at. And tho' a wise Woman will not value their Censure, yet she cares not to be the subject of their Discourse. The only way then is to retire from the World, as the *Israelites* did out of *Aegypt*, lest the Sacrifice we must make of its Follies shou'd provoke its Spleen.

This also puts us out of the road of Temptation, and very much redeems our Time, cutting off those extravagancies on which so much of it was squandred waay before, and furnishing us constantly with good employment, secures us from being seduc'd into bad. Great are the Benefits of holy Conversation which will be here enjoy'd; As Vice *is*, so Vertue *may* be catching; and to what heights of Piety will not she advance, who is plac'd where the sole business is to be Good, where there is no pleasure but in Religion, no contention but to excel in what is truly commendable; where her Soul is not defil'd nor her Zeal provok'd, by the sight or relation of those Villanies the World abounds with?

And by that Learning which will be here afforded, and that leisure we have to enquire after it, and to know and reflect on our own minds, we shall rescue our selves out of that woeful incogitancy we have slipt into, awaken our sleeping Powers, and make use of that reason which GOD has given us. We shall then begin to wonder at our Folly, that amongst all the pleasures we formerly pursued, we never attended to that most noble and

29

delicious one which is to be found in the chase of Truth; and bless our selves at last, that our eyes are open'd to discern, how much more pleasantly we may be entertain'd by our own Thoughts, than by all the Diversions which the world affords us. By this means we are fitted to receive the influences of the holy Spirit and are put in a due frame for Devotion. No doubt but He has often knock'd at the door of our hearts, when the croud and noise of our Vanities would not suffer us to regard or hear him, and could find no admittance when our house was so fill'd with other company. Here therefore is the fittest place for his Entertainment, for being freed from outward disturbances, we are entirely at leisure to attend so divine a Guest. Our Devotions will be perform'd with due attention, those Objects that used to distract being now remov'd from us; simplicity of desire will beget simplicity of thought, and that will make our mind most intense and elevated, when we come to address our selves to the Throne of Grace. Being dead to the things of this world, we shall with greatest fervour petition for those of another; and living always in a lively and awful sense of the divine Majesty, our hearts will ever be dispos'd to approach him in the most solemn, serious and reverent manner. 'Tis a very unseemly thing to jump from our Diversions to our Prayers; as if when we have been entertaining our selves and others with Vanity, we were instantly prepar'd to appear in the sacred presence of GOD. But a Religious Retirement and holy Conversation, will procure us a more serious Temper, a graver Spirit, and so both make us habitually fit to approach, and likewise stir us up to be more careful in our actual preparations when we do. For besides all other improvements of Knowledge, we shall hereby obtain truer Notions of GOD than we were capable of before, which is of very great consequence, since the want of right apprehensions concerning him, is the general cause of Mistakes in Religion, of Errors in Speculation, and Indecorums in Practice; for as GOD is the noblest Object of our Understanding, so nothing is more necessary or of such consequence to us as to busie our thoughts about him. And did we rightly consider his Nature, we should neither dare to forget him nor draw near to him with unclean hands and unholy hearts.

From this sacred Mountain where the world will be plac'd at our feet, at such a distance from us, that the steams of its corruptions shall not obscure our eye-sight, we shall have a right prospect of it and clearly discern that all its Allurements, all those Gaities and Pageantries, which at present we admire so much, are no better than insignificant Toys, which have no value but what our perverse Opinion imposes on them. Things which contribute so very little to our real Good, that even at *present*, which is their only season, we may live much happier without than with them; and which are so far from being necessary to our Felicity, that they shall vanish and be no more when that is consummate and perfect. Many are the Topics from whence we might declaim against the vanity of the world, but methinks Experience is so convincing that it supersedes all the rest, and wou'd certainly reclaim us from the immoderate love of earthly enjoyments, did we but seriously hearken to it. For tell me, Ladies, if your greatest Pleasures are not attended with a greater sting; when you think to grasp them, do they not either vanish into Air, or gall your fingers? To want or to enjoy them, is equally tormenting; the one produces in you the Pain of Hunger, the other of Loathing. For in reality, there is no good in them, nothing but the Shadow and appearance; if there were, you cou'd not so easily loath your old Delights and be so fond of variety, what is truly desirable never ending in disgust. They are not therefore Pleasures but Amusements which you now pursue, and which, through your ignorance of better Joys pretend to fill their place, toll you on with fair pretences and repay your Labour with defeated Hopes. Joys not near so lasting as the slightest toy you wear, the most capricious Humorist among you is more constant far than they. Come hither therefore and take a true view of 'em, that you may no longer deceive your selves with that which profits not, but spurning away these empty nothings, secure a portion in such a Bliss as will not fail, as cannot disappoint you! A Felicity which depending on GOD only and your own Minds, is out of Fortunes reach, will place you above the Batteries of the world, above its Terrors and Allurements, and enable you at once to triumph over and despise it. And what can be more glorious than to have a mind unshaken by the blandishments of Prosperity, or the rough shocks of Adversity; that passes thro' both with the same indifferency and integrity, is not to be tempted by either to a mean, unworthy and indecent Action?

Farther yet, besides that holy emulation which a continual view of the brightest and most exemplary Lives will excite in us, we shall have opportunity of contracting the purest and noblest Friendship; a Blessing, the purchase of which were richly worth all the World besides! For she who possesses a worthy Person, has certainly obtain'd the richest Treasure. A Blessing that Monarchs may envy, and she who enjoys is happier than she who fills a Throne! A Blessing, which next to the love of GOD, is the choicest Jewel in our Celestial Diadem; which, were it duly practis'd wou'd both fit us for Heav'n and bring it down into our hearts whilst we tarry here. For Friendship is a virtue which comprehends all the rest; none being fit for this, who is not adorn'd with every other Virtue. Probably one considerable cause of the degeneracy of the present Age, is the little true Friendship that is to be found in it; or perhaps you will rather say that this is the effect of our corruption. The cause and the effect are indeed reciprocal; for were the World better there wou'd be more Friendship, and were there more Friendship we should have a better World. But because *Iniquity abounds*, therefore the *love of many* is not only *waxen cold*, but quite benumb'd and perish'd. But if we have such narrow hearts, be so full of mistaken Self-love, so unreasonably fond of our selves, that we cannot spare a hearty Good-will to one or two choice Persons, how can it ever be thought, that we shou'd well acquit our selves of that Charity which is due to all Mankind? For Friendship is nothing else but Charity contracted; it is (in the words of an admired Author) a kind of revenging our selves on the narrowness of our Faculties, by exemplifying that extraordinary Charity on one or two, which we are willing, but not able to exercise towards all. And therefore 'tis without doubt the best Instructor to teach us our duty to our Neighbour, and a most excellent Monitor to excite us to make payment as far as our power will reach. It has a special force to dilate our hearts, to deliver them from that vicious *selfishness* and the rest of those sordid Passions which express a narrow illiberal temper, and are of such pernicious consequence to Mankind. That institution therefore must needs be highly beneficial, which both disposes us to be Friends our selves and helps to find them. But by Friendship I do not mean any thing like those intimacies that are abroad in the World, which are often combinations in evil and at best but insignificant dearnesses, as little resembling true Friendship, as Modern Practice does Primitive Christianity. But I intend by it the greatest usefulness, the most refin'd and dis-interest'd Benevolence, a love that thinks nothing within the bounds of Power and Duty, too much to do or suffer for its Beloved; And makes no distinction betwixt its Friend and its self, except that in Temporals it prefers her interest. But tho' it be very desirable to obtain such a Treasure, such a Medicine of Life as the wise man speaks, yet the Danger is great lest being deceiv'd in our choice, we suck in Poyson where we expected Health. And considering how apt we are to disguise our selves, how hard it is to know our own hearts much less anothers, it is not advisable to be too hasty in contracting so important a Relation; before that be done, it were well if we could look into the very Soul of the beloved Person, to discover what re-semblance it bears to our own, and in this Society we shall have the best opportunities of doing so. There are no Interests here to serve, no contrivances for another to be a stale to; the Souls of all the *Religious* will be open and free, and those par-ticular Friendships must be no prejudice to the general Amity. But yet, as in Heav'n that region of perfect Love, the happy Souls (as some are of opinion) now and then step aside from more general Conversations, to entertain themselves with a pecu-liar Friend; so, in this little emblem of that blessed place, what shou'd hinder, but that two Persons of a sympathizing disposition, the *make* and *frame* of whose Souls bears an exact conformity to each other, and therefore one wou'd think were purposely design'd by Heaven to unite and mix; what shou'd hinder them from entering into an holy combination to watch over each other for Good, to advise, encourage and direct, and to observe the minutest fault in order to its amendment. The truest effect of love being to endeavour the bettering the beloved Person. And there-fore nothing is more likely to improve us in Virtue, and advance us to the very highest pitch of Goodness than unfeigned Friend-ship, which is the most beneficial, as well as the most pleasant thing in the world.

But to hasten; such an Institution will much confirm us in Virtue and help us to persevere to the end, and by that sub-stantial Piety and solid Knowledge we shall here acquire, fit us to propagate Religion when we return into the World. An habitual Practice of Piety for some years will so root and establish us in it, that Religion will become a second Nature, and we must do strange violences to our selves, if after that we dare venture to oppose it. For besides all the other Advantages that Virtue has over Vice, this will disarm it of *Custom*, the only thing that recommends it, bravely win its strongest Fort and turn its own Cannon against it self. How almost impossible wou'd it be for her to sin, whose *Understanding* being clearly illuminated with the knowledge of the Truth, is too wise to be impos'd on by those false Representations that sin wou'd deceive it with; whose *Will* has found out and united it self to its true Centre; and having been long habituated to move in a right line, has no temptation to decline to an Oblique. Whose *Affections* have daily regaled on those delicious Fruits of Paradise which Religion presents them with, and are therefore too sublime and refin'd to relish the muddy Pleasures of sensual Delights. It must certainly be a Miracle if such an one relinquish her Glory and Joy; she must be as bad as *Lucifer* himself, who after such Enjoyments can forsake her Heaven. 'Tis too unreasonable to imagine such an Apostacy, the supposition is monstrous and therefore we may conclude will never or very rarely happen. And then what a blessed World shou'd we have, shining with so many stars of *Vertue*, who not content to be happy themselves alone, for that's a narrowness of mind too much beneath their God-like temper, would like the glorious Lights of Heaven, or rather like him who made them, diffuse their benign Influences wherever they come. Having gain'd an entrance into Paradise themselves, they wou'd both shew the way, and invite others to partake of their felicity. Instead of that Froth and Impertinence, that Censure and Pragmaticalness, with which Feminine Conversations so much abound, we should hear their tongues employ'd in making Proselytes to heaven, in running down Vice, in establishing Virtue and proclaiming their Maker's Glory. 'Twou'd be more genteel to give and take instructions about the ornaments of the Mind, than to enquire after the Mode; and a Lecture on the Fashions wou'd become as disagreeable as at present any serious discourse is. Not the Follies of the Town, but the Beauties and the Love of JESUS wou'd be the most polite and delicious Entertainments. 'Twould be thought as rude and barbarous to send our Visitors away uninstructed, as our foolishness at present reckons it to introduce a pertinent and useful Conversation. Ladies of Quality wou'd be able to distinguish themselves from their Inferiors, by the blessings they communicated and the good they did. For this is their grand Prerogative, their *distinguishing Character*, that they are plac'd in a condition which makes that which is every ones *Chief* business, to be their *Only* employ. They have nothing to do but to glorifie GOD, and to benefit their Neighbours, and she who does not thus improve her Talent, is more vile and despicable than the meanest Creature that attends her.

And if after so many Spiritual Advantages, it be convenient to mention Temporals, here Heiresses and Persons of Fortune may be kept secure from the rude attempts of designing Men; And she who has more Money than Discretion, need not curse her Stars for being expos'd a prey to bold importunate and rapacious Vultures. She will not here be inveigled and impos'd on, will neither be bought nor sold, nor be forc'd to marry for her own quiet, when she has no inclination to it, but what the being tir'd out with a restless importunity occasions. Or if she be dispos'd to marry, here she may remain in safety till a convenient Match be offer'd by her Friends, and be freed from the danger of a dishonourable one. Modesty requiring that a Woman should not love before Marriage, but only make choice of one whom she can love hereafter; She who has none but innocent affections, being easily able to fix them where Duty requires.

And though at first I propos'd to my self to speak nothing in particular of the employment of the *Religious*, yet to give a Specimen how useful they will be to the World, I am now inclin'd to declare, that it is design'd a part of their business shall be to give the best Education to the Children of Persons of Quality, who shall be attended and instructed in lesser Matters by meaner Persons deputed to that Office, but the forming of their minds shall be the particular care of those of their own Rank, who cannot have a more pleasant and useful employment than to exercise and encrease their own knowledge, by instilling it into these young ones, who are most like to profit under such Tutors. For how can their little Pupils forbear to credit them, since they do not decry the World (as others may be thought to do) because they could not enjoy it, but when they had it in their power, were courted and caress'd by it, for very good Reasons and on mature deliberation, thought fit to relinquish and despise its offers for a better choice? Nor are mercenary people on other accounts capable of doing so much good to young Persons; because having often but short views of things themselves, sordid and low Spirits, they are not like to form a generous temper in the minds of the Educated. Doubtless 'twas well consider'd of him, who wou'd not trust the breeding of his Son to a Slave, because no thing great or excellent could be expected from a person of that condition.

And when by the increase of their Revenue, the *Religious* are enabled to do such a work of Charity, the Education they design to bestow on the Daughters of Gentlemen who are fallen into decay will be no inconsiderable advantage to the Nation. For hereby many Souls will be preserv'd from great Dishonours and put in a comfortable way of subsisting, being either receiv'd into the House if they incline to it, or otherwise dispos'd of. It being suppos'd that prudent Men will reckon the endowments they here acquire a sufficient *Dowry*, and that a discreet and vertuous Gentlewoman will make a better Wife than she whose mind is empty tho her Purse be full.

But some will say, May not People be good without this confinement? may they not live at large in the World, and yet serve GOD as acceptably as here? 'Tis allow'd they may; truly wise and virtuous Souls will do it by the assistance of GOD's Grace in despite of all temptations; and I heartily wish that all Women were of this temper. But it is to be consider'd, that there are *tender* Virtues who need to be screened from the ill Airs of the World: many persons who had *begun* well might have gone to the Grave in peace and innocence, had it not been their misfortune to be violently tempted. For those who have honest Hearts have not always the strongest Heads; and sometimes the enticements of the World and the subtil insinuations of such as lie in wait to deceive, may make their Heads giddy, stagger their Resolutions, and overthrow all the fine hopes of a promising beginning. 'Tis fit therefore, such tender *Cyons* shou'd be transplanted, that they may be supported by the prop of Virtuous Friendship, and confirm'd in Goodness by holy Examples, which alas! they will not often meet with in the World.

And, such is the weakness of humane Nature, bad People are not so apt to be better'd by the Society of the Good, as the Good are to be corrupted by theirs. Since therefore we daily pray against temptation, it cannot be amiss if we take all prudent care to avoid it, and not out of a vain presumption face the danger which GOD may justly permit to overcome us for a due correction of our Pride. It is not impossible for a man to live in an infected House or Town and escape with Life and Health, yet if he have a place in the Country to retire to, he will not make slight of that advantage; and surely the Health of our Souls is of greater consideration than the health of our Bodies. Besides, she has need of an establish'd Virtue and consummated Prudence, who so well understands the great end for which she came into the World, and so faithfully pursues it, that not content to be wise and good her self alone, she endeavours to propagate Wisdom and Piety to all within her Sphere; But neither this Prudence nor heroic Goodness are easily attainable amidst the noise and hurry of the World, we must therefore retire a while from its clamour and importunity, if we generously design to do it good, and having calmly and sedately observ'd and rectify'd what is amiss in our selves, we shall be fitter to promote a Reformation in others. A devout Retirement will not only strengthen and confirm our Souls, that they be not infected by the worlds Corruptions, but likewise so purify and refine them, that they will become Antidotes to expel the Poyson in others, and spread a salutary Air on ev'ry Side.

If any object against a Learned Education, that it will make Women vain and assuming, and instead of correcting encrease their Pride: I grant that a smattering in Learning may, for it has this effect on the Men, none so Dogmatical and so forward to shew their Parts as your little *Pretenders* to Science. But I wou'd not have the Ladies content themselves with the *shew*, my desire is that they shou'd not rest till they obtain the *Substance*. And then, she who is most knowing will be forward to own with the wise *Socrates* that she knows nothing: nothing that is matter of Pride and Ostentation; nohing but what is attended with so much ignorance and imperfection, that it cannot reasonably elate and puff her up. The more she knows, she will be the less subject to talkativeness and its sister Vices, because she discerns, that the most difficult piece of Learning is to know when to use and when to hold ones Tongue, and never to speak but to the purpose.

But the men if they rightly understand their own interest, have no reason to oppose an ingenious Education of the Women, since 'twou'd go a great way towards reclaiming the men. Great is the influence we have over them in their Childhood, in which time if a Mother be discreet and knowing as well as devout, she has many opportunities of giving such a *Form* and *Season* to the tender Mind of the Child, as will shew its good effects thro' all the stages of his Life. But tho' you should not allow her capable of doing *good*, 'tis certain she may do *hurt:* if she do not *make* the Child, she has power to *marr* him, by suffering her fondness to get the better of discreet affection. But besides this, a good and prudent Wife wou'd wonderfully work on an ill man; he must be a Brute indeed, who cou'd hold out against all those innocent Arts, those gentle persuasives and obliging methods she wou'd use to reclaim him. Piety is often offensive when it is accompanied with indiscretion; but she who is as Wise as Good, possesses such Charms as can hardly fail of prevailing. Doubtless her Husband is a much happier Man and more likely to abandon all his ill Courses than he who has none to come home to, and an ignorant, froward and fantastick Creature. An ingenious Conversation will make his life comfortable, and he who can be so well entertain'd at home, needs not run into Temptations in search of Diversions abroad. The only danger is that the Wife be more knowing than the Husband; but if she be 'tis his own fault, since he wants no opportunities of improvement; unless he be a natural *Block-head*, and then such an one will need a wise Woman to govern him, whose prudence will conceal it from publick Observation, and at once both cover and supply his defects. Give me leave therefore to hope, that no Gentleman who has honourable designs, will hence-forward decry Knowledge and Ingenuity in her he would pretend to Honour; If he does, it may serve for a Test to distinguish the feigned and unworthy from the real Lover.

Now who that has a spark of Piety will go about to oppose so Religious a design? What generous Spirit that has a due regard to the good of Mankind, will not be forward to advance and perfect it? Who will think 500 pounds too much to lay out for the purchase of so much Wisdom and Happiness? Certainly we shou'd not think them too dearly paid for by a much greater Sum, did not our pitiful and sordid Spirits set a much higher value on Money than it deserves. But granting so much of that dear Idol were given away, a person thus bred, will easily make it up by her Frugality and other Virtues; if she bring less, she will not waste so much as others do in superfluous and vain Expences. Nor can I think of any expedient so useful as this to Persons of Quality who are over-stock'd with Children, for thus they may honourably dispose of them without impairing their Estates. Five or six hundred pounds may be easily spar'd with a daughter, when so many thousands would go deep; and yet as the world goes be a very inconsiderable Fortune for Ladies of their Birth, neither maintain them in that *Port* which Custom makes almost necessary, nor procure them an equal Match, those of their own Rank (contrary to the generous custom of the *Germans*) chusing rather to fill their Coffers than to preserve the purity of their Blood, and therefore think a weighty Bag the best Gentility, preferring a wealthy Upstart before the best Descended and best Qualified Lady; their own extravagancies perhaps having made it necessary, that they may keep up an empty shadow of Greatness, which is all that remains to shew what their Ancestors have been.

Does any think their Money lost to their Families when 'tis put in here? I will only ask what course they can take to save it, and at once to preserve their Money, their Honour and their Daughters too? Were they sure the Ladies wou'd die unmarried, I shou'd commend their Thrift, but Experience has too often shewn us the vanity of this expectation. For the poor Lady having past the prime of her Years in Gaity and Company, in running the Circle of all the Vanities of the Town, having spread all her Nets and us'd all her Arts for Conquest, and finding that the Bait fails where she wou'd have it take; and having all this while been so over-careful of her Body, that she had no time to improve her Mind, which therefore affords her no safe retreat, now she meets with Disappointments abroad, and growing every day more and more sensible that the respect which us'd to be paid her decays as fast as her Beauty; quite terrified with the dreadful Name of *Old Maid*, which yet none but Fools will reproach her with, nor any wise Woman be afraid of; to avoid this terrible *Mormo*, and the scoffs that are thrown on superannuated Virgins, she flies to some dishonourable Match as her last, tho' much mistaken Refuge, to the disgrace of her Family and her own irreparable Ruin. And now let any Person of Honour tell me, if it were not richly worth some thousand Pounds, to prevent all this mischief, and the having an idle Fellow, and perhaps a race of beggarly Children to hang on him and to provide for?

Cou'd I think of any other Objection I wou'd consider it; there's nothing indeed which witty Persons may not argue *for* and *against*, but they who duly weigh the Arguments on both sides, unless they be extreamly prejudiced, will easily discern the great usefulness of this Institution. The *Beaux* perhaps, and topping Sparks of the Town will ridicule and laugh at it. For Virtue her self as bright as she is, can't escape the lash of scurrilous Tongues; the comfort is, whilst they impotently endeavour to throw dirt on her, they are unable to foil her Beauty, and only defile and render themselves the more contemptible. They may therefore if they please, hug themselves in their own dear folly, and enjoy the diversion of their own insipid Jests. She has but little Wisdom and less Virtue, who is to be frightned from what she judges reasonable, by the scoffs and insignificant noises of ludicrous Wits and pert Buffoons. And no wonder that such as they who have nothing to shew for their pretences to Wit, but some scraps of Plays and blustring Nonsense; who fancy a well adjusted Peruke is able to supply their want of Brains, and that to talk *much* is a sign of ingenuity, tho't be never so little to the purpose, no wonder that they object against our *Proposal*: 'Twou'd indeed spoil the Trade of the gay fluttering Fops, who wou'd be at a loss, had they no body as impertinent as themselves to talk with. The Criticism of their Dress wou'd be useless, and the labour of their *Valet de Chambre* lost, unless they cou'd peaceably lay aside their Rivalling, and one Ass be content to complement and admire another. For the Ladies wou'd have more discernment than to esteem a Man for such Follies as shou'd rather incline them to scorn and despise him. They wou'd never be so sottish as to imagine, that he who regards nothing but his own brutish Appetite, shou'd have any real affection for them, nor ever expect Fidelity from one who is unfaithful to GOD and his own Soul. They wou'd not be so absurd as to suppose, that Man can esteem them who neglects his Maker; for what are all those fine Idolatries, by which he wou'd recommend himself to his pretended Goddess, but mockery and delusion from him who forgets and affronts the true Deity? They wou'd not value themselves on account of the Admiration of such incompetent Judges, nor consequently make use of those little trifling Arts that are necessary to recommend them to such Admirers; Neither wou'd they give them opportunity to profess themselves their Slaves so long till at last they become their Masters.

What now remains, but to reduce to Practice that which tends so very much to our advantage. Is Charity so dead in the world that none will contribute to the saving their own and their neighbours Souls? Shall we freely expend our Money to purchase Vanity, and often times both present and future Ruin, and find none for such an eminent good Work, which will make the Ages to come arise and call us Blessed? I wou'd fain Persuade my self better things, and that I shall one day see this *Religious Retirement* happily settled, and its great designs wisely and vigorously pursu'd; and methinks I have already a Vision of that lustre and glory our Ladies cast far and near; Let me therefore intreat the rest of our Sex, who tho' at liberty in the world, are the miserable Slaves of their own vile affections, let me intreat them to lay aside their Prejudices and whatever borders on Envy and Malice, and with impartial eyes to behold the Beauties of our *Religious*. The native innocency and un-affectedness of whose Charms, and the unblameable Integrity of their Lives, are abundantly more taking than all the curious Artifices and studied Arts the other can invent to recommend them, even bad men themselves being Judges, who often betray a secret Veneration for that virtue they wou'd seem to despise and endeavour to corrupt. As there is not any thing, no not the least shadow of a motive to recommend Vice but its fashion-ableness and the being accustom'd to it, so there is nothing at all forbidding in Virtue but her uncouthness. Acquaint your selves with her a little, and you'll wonder how you cou'd be so foolish as to delight in any thing besides! For you'll find her Conversation most sweet and obliging; her Precepts most easy and beneficial; her very tasks Joys, and her Injunctions the highest Pleasures. She will not rob you of any innocent delight, nor engage you to any thing beneath your Birth and Breeding; but will put a new and more grateful relish into all your Enjoyments, and make them more delicious with her Sweetness. She'll preserve and augment your Honour, by allying you to the King of Heaven; secure your Grandeur by fixing it on a firm bottom, such as the caprice of Fortune cannot shake or overthrow; she'll enlarge your Souls, raise them above the common level, and encourage that allowable Pride of Scorning to do a base unworthy action; Make you truly amiable in the eyes of GOD and Man, preserve even the Beauty of your Bodies as long as 'tis possible for such a brittle thing to last, and when it must of necessity decay, impress such a loveliness on your Minds as will shine thro' and brighten your very Countenances; enriching you with such a stock of Charms, that Time which devours every other thing, shall never be able to decay: In a word, 'tis Virtue only which can make you truly happy in *this* world as well as in the next.

There is a sort of Bravery and Greatness of Soul, which does more truly ennoble us than the highest Title, and it consists in living up to the dignity of our Natures, being so sensible of our own worth as to think our selves too great to do a degenerate and unbecoming thing; in passing indifferently thro' Good and Evil Fortune, without being corrupted by the one or deprest by the other. For she that can do so, gives evidence that her Happiness depends not on so mutable a thing as this World; but, in a due subserviency to the Almighty, is bottom'd only on her own great Mind. This is the richest Ornament, and renders a Woman glorious in the lowest Fortune. So shining is real worth, that like a Diamond it loses not its lustre tho' cast on a Dunghill. Whereas, she who is advanc'd to some eminent Station and wants this natural and solid Greatness, is no better than Fortunes *May-game*, rendered more conspicuous that she may appear the more contemptible. Let those therefore who value themselves only on external accomplishments, consider how liable they are to decay, and how soon they may be depriv'd of them, and that supposing they shou'd continue, they are but sandy Foundations to build Esteem upon. What a disappointment will it be to a Ladies Admirer as well as to her self, that her Conversation shou'd lose or endanger the Victory her eyes had gain'd! For when the Passion of a Lover is Exchang'd for the

Indifference of a Husband, and a frequent review has lessen'd the wonder which her Charms at first has rais'd, she'll retain no more than such a formal respect as decency and good breeding will require, and perhaps hardly that, but unless he be a very good Man (and indeed the world is not over full of 'em) her worthlessness has made a forfeit of his Affections, which are seldom fixt by any other thing than Veneration and Esteem. Whereas a wise and good Woman is useful and valuable in all Ages and Conditions: she who chiefly attends the *one thing needful*, the *good part which shall not be taken from her*, lives a cheerful and pleasant Life, innocent and sedate, calm and tranquill, and makes a glorious Exit; being translated from the most happy life on Earth to unspeakable happiness in Heaven; a fresh and fragrant Name embalming her Dust, and extending its Perfume to succeeding Ages. Whilst the Fools, and the worst sort of them the wicked, *live* as well as *die* in Misery, go out in a snuff, leaving nothing but stench and putrefaction behind them.

To close all, if this *Proposal* which is but a rough draught and rude Essay, and which might be made much more beautiful by a better Pen, give occasion to wiser heads to improve and perfect it, I have my end. For imperfect as it is, it seems so desirable, that she who drew the Scheme is full of hopes, it will not want kind hands to perform and compleat it. But if it miss of that, it is but a few hours thrown away and a little labour in vain, which yet will not be lost, if what is here offer'd may serve to express her hearty good-will, and how much she desires your Improvement, who is

LADIES,
Your very humble Servant.

FINIS.

A Serious

P R O P O S A L

TO THE

L A D I E S

PART II:

Wherein a Method is offer'd

for the Improvement

of their Minds.

LONDON:

Printed for *Richard Wilkin* at
the *King's Head* in *St. Paul's*
Church-yard, 1697.

To her Royal Highness
THE
Princess ANN of Denmark

MADAM,

What was at first adress'd to the Ladies in General, *as seeming not considerable enough to appear in your Royal Highnesses Presence, not being ill receiv'd by them, and having got the Addition of a Second Part, now presumes on a more* Particular *Application to Her who is the Principal of them, and whose Countenance and Example may reduce to Practice, what it can only Advise and Wish.*

And when I consider you Madam as a Princess who is sensible that the Chief Prerogative of the great is the Power they have of doing more Good than those in an Inferior Station can, I see no cause to fear that your Royal Highness will deny Encouragement to that which has no other Design than the Bettering of the World, expecially the most neglected part of it as to all Real Improvement, the Ladies. It is by the Exercise of this Power that Princes become truly Godlike, they are never so illustrious as when they shine as Lights in the World by an Eminent and Heroic Vertue. A Vertue as much above Commendation as it is above Detraction, which sits equally Silent and Compos'd when Opprest with Praises or Pursu'd with Calumnys, is neither hurt by these nor better'd by the other; for the Service of GOD, and the Resembling Him, being its only Aim, His Approbation in a soft and inward Whisper, is more than the loud Huzza's and Plaudits of ten thousand Worlds.

I shall not therefore offend your Royal Ear with the nauseous strain of Dedications; for what can one say, when by how much the more any Person deserves Panegyric, by so much the less they endure it? That your Royal Highness may be All that is

47

truly Great and Good, and have a Confluence of Temporal, Sanctify'd and Crown'd with Spiritual and Eternal Blessings, is the unfeigned and constant desire of

MADAM,

Your Royal Highnesses

Most Humble and most

Obedient Servant.

THE
CONTENTS
Of the Second Part.

The
INTRODUCTION,
Containing a farther
PERSWASIVE
TO THE
L A D I E S
To endeavour the
Improvement of their Minds

DID the Author of the former Essay towards th' Improvement of the Ladies consult her own Reputation only, she wou'd not hazard it once more, by treating on so nice a Subject in a Curious and Censorious Age, but content her self with the favourable reception which the good natur'd part of the World were pleased to afford to her first Essay. It is not unusual she knows for Writers to mind no more than their own Credit, to be pleas'd if they can make a handsom florish, get a Name amongst the Authors, come off with but a little Censure and some Commendations. Or if there are a few generous Souls who are got above the Hope or Fear of vulgar breath, who don't much regard that Applause which is dispenc'd more commonly by Fancy or Passion than by Judgment; they rest satisfied however in a good Intention, and comfort themselves that they've endeavour'd the Reformation of the Age, let those look to't who will not follow their Advices. But give her leave to profess, that as she is very indifferent what the Critics say, if the Ladies receive any Advantage by her attempts to serve them, so it will give her the greatest uneasiness if having prov'd that they are capable of the best things, she can't perswade to a pursuit of them. It were more to her Satisfaction to find her Project condemn'd as foolish and impertinent, than to find it receiv'd with some Approbation, and yet no body endeavouring to put it in Practice. Since the former wou'd only reproach her own Understanding, but the latter is a shame to Mankind, as being a plain sign that tho they discern and commend what is Good, they have not the Vertue and Courage to Act accordingly.

And can you Ladies deny her so cheap a Reward for all the Good will she bears you, as the Pleasure of seeing you Wise and Happy? Can you envy her the Joy of assisting at *Your* Triumphs? for if ever she contend for Laurels it shall be only to lay them at the Ladies feet. Why won't you begin to think, and no longer dream away your Time in a wretched incogitancy? Why does not a generous Emulation fire your hearts and inspire you with Noble and Becoming Resentments? The Men of Equity are so just as to confess the errors which the Proud and Inconsiderate had imbib'd to your prejudice, and that if you allow them the preference in Ingenuity, it is not because you *must*, but because you *will*. Can you be in Love with servitude and folly? Can you dote on a mean, ignorant and ignoble Life? An Ingenious Woman is no Prodigy to be star'd on, for you have it in your power to inform the World, that you can every one of you be so, if you please your selves. It is not enough to wish and to would it, or t'afford a faint Encomium upon what you pretend is beyond your Power; Imitation is the heartiest Praise you can give, and is a Debt which Justice requires to be paid to every worthy Action. What Sentiments were fit to be rais'd in you to day ought to remain to morrow, and the best Commendation you can bestow on a Book is immediately to put it in Practice; otherwise you become self condemn'd, your Judgment reproaches your Actions, and you live a contradiction to your selves. If you *approve*, Why don't you *follow*? And if you *Wish*, Why shou'd you not *Endeavour*? especially since that wou'd reduce your Wishes to Act, and make you of Wellwishers to Vertue and Good sense, become glorious Examples of them.

And pray what is't that hinders you? The singularity of the Matter? Are you afraid of being out of the ordinary way and therefore admir'd and gaz'd at? Admiration does not use to be uneasy to our Sex; a great many Vanities might be spar'd if we consulted only our own conveniency and not other peoples Eyes and Sentiments: And why shou'd that which usually recommends a trifling Dress, deter us from a real Ornament? Is't not as fine to be first in this as well as any other Fashion? Singularity is indeed to be avoided except in matters of importance, in such a case why shou'd not we assert our Liberty, and not suffer every Trifler to impose a Yoke of Impertinent Customs on us? She who forsakes the Path to which Reason directs is much to blame, but she shall never do any thing Praise-worthy and excellent who is not got above unjust Censures, and too steady and well resolv'd to be sham'd from her Duty by the empty Laughter of such as have nothing but airy Noise and Confidence to recommend them. Firmness and strength of Mind will carry us thro all these little persecutions, which may create us some uneasiness for a while, but will afterwards end in our Glory and Triumph.

Is it the difficulty of attaining the Bravery of the Mind, the Labour and Cost that keeps you from making a purchase of it? Certainly they who spare neither Money nor Pains t'obtain a gay outside and make a splendid appearance, who can get over so many difficulties, rack their brains, lay out their time and thoughts in contriving, stretch their Relations Purses in procuring, nay and rob the very Poor, to whom the Overplus of a full Estate, after the owners Necessaries and decent Conveniencies according to her Quality are supplied, is certainly due, they who can surmount so many difficulties, cannot have the face to pretend any here. Labour is sweet when there's hope of success, and the thing labour'd after is Beautiful and Desireable: And if Wisdom be not so I know not what is; if it is not worth while to procure such a temper of mind as will make us happy in all Conditions, there's nothing worth our Thoughts and Care, 'tis best to fold our hands with *Solomon's* Sluggard and sleep away the remainder of a useless and wretched Life.

And that success will not be wanting to our Endeavours if we heartily use them, was design'd to be evinc'd in the former Essay, and I hope I have not lost my Point, but that the Theory is sufficiently establish'd; and were there but a General Attempt, the Practice wou'd be so visible that I suppose there wou'd remain no more place to dispute it. But this is your Province Ladies: For tho I desire your improvement never so passionately, tho I shou'd have prov'd it feasible with the clearest Demonstration, and more proper for you to set about; yet if you *will* believe it impossible, and upon that or any other prejudice forbear t'attempt it, I'm like to go without my Wishes; my Arguments what ever they may be in themselves, are weak and impertinent to you, because you make them useless and defeat them of the End they aim at. But I hope better things of you; I dare say you understand your own interest too well to neglect it so grossly and have a greater share of sense, whatever some Men affirm, than to be content to be kept any longer under their Tyranny in Ignorance and Folly, since it is in your Power to regain your Freedom, if you please but t'endeavour it. I'm unwilling to believe there are any among you who are obstinately bent against what is praise-worthy in themselves, and Envy or Detract from it in others; who won't allow any of their Sex a capacity to write Sense, because they want it, or exert their Spleen where they ought to shew their Kindness or Generous Emulation; who sicken at their Neighbours Vertues, or think anothers Praises a lessening of their Character; or meanly satisfie ill-nature by a dull Malicious Jest at what deserves to be approv'd and imitated. No Ladies, Your Souls are certainly of a better Make and Nobler temper, your Industry is never exerted to pull down others but to rise above them, the only Resentment that arises at your Neighbours Commendations is a harmless blush for your own Idleness in letting them so far outstrip you, and a generous Resolution to repair your former neglects by future diligence; One need not fear offending you by commending an other Lady in your Presence, or that it shou'd be thought an affront or defect in good breeding to give them their lawful Eulogies: You have too just a Sentiment of your own Merit to envy or detract from others, for no Body's addicted to these little Vices but they who are diffident of their own worth; You know very well 'tis infinitely better to *be* good than to *seem* so, and that true Vertue has Beauty enough in her self t'attract our hearts and engage us in her service, tho she were neglected and despis'd by all the World. 'Tis this therefore you endeavour after, 'tis the approbation of GOD and your own Consciences you mainly esteem, which you find most ascertain'd by an humble Charity, and that you never merit Praise so much, because you never make so great a progress in which is truly praise-worthy, as when your own defects are often in your eyes t'excite you to watch against and amend them, and other peoples Vertues continually represented before you in their brightest lustre, to the end you may aspire to equal or surpass them.

I suppose than that you're fill'd with a laudable Ambition to brighten and enlarge your Souls, that the Beauty of your Bodies is but a secondary care, your Dress grows unconcerning, and your Glass is ne're consulted but in such little intervals of time as hang loose between those hours that are destin'd to nobler Employments; you now begin to throw off your old Prejudices and smile on 'em as antiquated Garbs; false Reasoning won't down with you, and glittering Non-sense tho address'd to your selves in the specious appearance of Respect and Kindness, has lost is *haut goust;* Wisdom is thought a better recommendation than Wit, and Piety than a *Bon-mien;* you esteem a Man only as he is an admirer of Vertue, and not barely for that he is yours; Books are now become the finest Ornaments of your Closets, and Contemplation the most agreeable Entertainment of your leisure hours; your Friendships are not cemented by Intrigues nor spent in vain Diversions, but in the search of Knowledge, and acquisition of Vertuous Habits, a mutual Love to which was the Origin of 'em; nor are any Friends so acceptable as those who tell you faithfully of your faults and take the properest method to amend 'em. How much better are you entertain'd now your Conversations are pertinent and ingenious, and that Wisdom never fails to make one in your Visits? Solitude is no more insupportable; you've conquered that silly dread of being afraid to be alone, since Innocence is the safest Guard, and no Company can be so desirable as GOD's and his holy Angels conversing with an upright mind; your Devotion is a Rational service, not the repetition of a Set of good words at a certain season; you read and you delight in it, because it informs your Judgments, and furnishes Materials for your thoughts to work on; and you love your Religion and make it your Choice because you understand it; the only Conquest you now design and lay out your care to obtain is over Vice and Prophaness; you study to engage men in the love of true Piety and Goodness, and no farther to be Lovers of

your selves than as you are the most amiable and illustrious examples of 'em; you find your Wit has lost nothing of its salt and
agreeableness by being employ'd about its proper business, the
exposing Folly; your Raillery is not a whit less pleasant for being
more Charitable, and you can render Vice as ridiculous as you
please, without exposing those unhappy Persons who're guilty
of it; your Humour abates not of its innocent gaity now that it
is more upon the Guard, for you know very well that true Joy is
a sedate and solid thing, a tranquility of mind, not a boisterous
and empty flash: Instead of Creditors your doors are fill'd with
indigent Petitioners who don't so often go without your Bounty
as the other us'd to do without their just demands; nor are you
unjust to some under colour of being Charitable to others, and
when you give Liberally, give no more than what is lawfully
your own. You disdain the base ungenerous Practice of pretending Kindness where you really mean none; and of making a poor
Country Lady less instructed in the formalities of the Town
than your selves, pay sufficiently for your seeming Civility and
kind Entertainment by becoming the Subject of your mirth and
diversion as soon as she is gone; but one may now pretty securely
relie on your Sincerity, for when this lower sort of Treachery
is abhorr'd, there can certainly be no place for that more abom-
inable one of betraying and seducing unwary Innocence. I do
not question Ladies but that this is the Practice of the greatest
number of you, and would be of all the rest were it not for some
little discouragements they meet with, which really are not so
great as their own modesty and diffidence of themselves represent 'em. They think they've been bred up in Idleness and Impertinence, and study will be irksome to them, who have never
employ'd their mind to any good purpose, and now when they
wou'd they want the method of doing it; they know not how to
look into their Souls, or if they do, they find so many disorders
to be rectified, so many wants to be supplied, that frighted with
the difficulty of the work they lay aside the thoughts of under-
taking it. They have been barbarously us'd, their Education and
greatest Concerns neglected, whilst their imprudent Parents and
Guardians were busied in managing their Fortunes and regulat-
ing their Mien; who so their Purse was full and their outside

plausible, matter'd not much the poverty and narrowness of their minds, have taught them perhaps to repeat their Catechism and a few good Sentences, to read a Chapter and *say* their Prayers, tho perhaps with as little Understanding as a Parrot, and fancied that this was Charm enough to secure them against the temptations of the present world and to waft them to a better; and so thro want of use and by misapplying their Thoughts to trifles and impertinencies, they've perhaps almost lost those excellent Capacities which probably were afforded them by nature for the highest things. For such as these I've a world of Kindness and Compassion, I regret their misfortune as much as they can themselves, and suppose they're willing to repair it and very desirous to inform themselves were't not for the shame of confessing their Ignorance. But let me intreat them to consider that there's no Ignorance so shameful, no Folly so absurd as that which refuses Instruction, be it upon what account it may. All good Persons will pity not upbraid their former unhappiness, as not being their own but other Peoples fault; whereas they themselves are responsible if they continue it, since that's an Evidence that they are silly and despicable, not because they *cou'd* not, but because they *wou'd* not be better Informed. But where is the shame of being taught? for who is there that does not need it? Alas, Human Knowledge is at best defective, and always progressive, so that she who knows the most has only this advantage, that she has made a little more speed than her Neighbours. And what's the Natural Inference from hence? Not to give out, but to double our diligence; perhaps we may out-strip 'em, as the Penitent often does him who needs no Repentance. The worst that can be is the perishing in a glorious attempt, and tho we shou'd happen to prove successless, 'tis yet worth our while to've had such a noble design. But there's no fear of ill success if we are not wanting to our selves, an honest and laborious mind may perform all things. Indeed an affected Ignorance, a humorous delicacy and niceness which will not speculate a notion for fear of spoiling a look, nor think a serious thought lest she shou'd damp the gaity of her humour; she who is so top full of her outward excellencies, so careful that every look, every motion, every thing about her shou'd appear in Form, as she employs her Thoughts to a very pitiful use, so is she almost past hopes of recovery, at least so long as she continues this humour, and does not grow a little less concern'd for her Body that she may attend her Mind. Our directions are thrown away upon such a temper, 'tis to no purpose to harp to an Ass, or to chant forth our Charms in the Ears of a deaf Adder; but I hope there are none so utterly lost in folly and impertinence: If there are, we can only afford them our Pity for our Advice will do no good.

As for those who are desirous to improve and only want to be assisted and put into the best method of doing it, somewhat was attempted in order to do them that service in the former Essay, in which they may please to remember that having remov'd that groundless prejudice against an ingenious Education of the Women, which is founded upon supposition of the impossibility or uselessness of it, and having assign'd the reasons why they are so little improv'd, since they are so capable of improvement, and since 'tis so necessary that others as well as themselves shou'd endeavour it; which reaons are chiefly Ill-nurture, Custom, loss of Time, the want of Retirement, or of knowing how to use it, so that by the disuse of our Faculties we seem to have lost them if we ever had any; are sunk into an Animal life wholly taken up with sensible objects; either have no Ideas of the most necessary things or very *false* ones; and run into all those mischiefs which are the natural Consequences of such mismanagement; we then proceeded to propose a remedy for these Evils, which we affirm'd cou'd hardly be rectified but by erecting a Seminary where Ladies might be duly Educated, and we hope our Proposition was such that all impartial Readers are convinc'd it wou'd answer the Design, that is, tend very much to the real advantage and improvement of the Ladies. In order to which it was in general propos'd to acquaint them with Judicious Authors, give them opportunity of Retirement and Recollection and put them in a way of Ingenious Conversation, whereby they might enlarge their prospect, rectify their false Ideas, form in their Minds adequate conceptions of the End and Dignity of their Natures, not only have the Name and common Principles of Religion floating in their Heads and sometimes running out at their Mouths, but understand the design and meaning of it, and have a just apprehension, a lively sentiment of its Beauties and Excellencies; know wherein the Nature of a true Christian consists; and not only feel Passions, but be able to direct and regulate their Motions; have a true Notion of the Nothingness of Material things and of the reality and substantialness of immaterial, and consequently contemn this present World as it deserves, fixing all their Hopes upon and exerting all their Endeavours to obtain the Glories of the next. But because this was only propos'd in general, and the particular method of effecting it left to the Discretion of those who shou'd Govern and Manage the Seminary, without which we are still of Opinion that the Interest of the Ladies can't be duly serv'd, yet in the mean time till that can be erected and that nothing in our power may be wanting to do them service, we shall attempt to lay down in this second part some more minute Directions, and such as we hope if attended to may be of use to them.

The
SECOND PART
Of The
P R O P O S A L
TO THE
L A D I E S

CHAP. I.

*Of the Mutual Relation between Ignorance and Vice, and
Knowledge and Purity.*

WHAT are Ignorance and Vice but Diseases of the Mind contracted in its two principal Faculties the Understanding and Will? And such too as like many Bodily distempers do mutually foment each other. Ignorance disposes to Vice, and Wickedness reciprocally keeps us Ignorant, so that we cannot be free from the one unless we cure the other; the former part of this Proposition Part I. has been already shewn, and the latter may easily be made apparent; page 7, &c for as every Plant does Naturally draw such juices towards it as serve for its Nutrition, as every Creature has an aptness to take such courses as tend to its preservation; so Vice that spawn of the Devil, that *Ignis fatuus* which can't subsist but in the dark night of Ignorance, casts forth Vapours and Mists to darken the Soul and eclipse the clear light of Knowledge from her view. And tho a Wicked Man may pretend to Wit, tho he have never so much Acumen and Facetiousness of Humour, yet his Impiety proclaims his Folly; he may have a lively Fancy, an Intriguing Cunning and Contrivance, and so may an Ape or a Fox, who probably if they had but Speech, tho destitute of Reason, wou'd outdo him in his own way; but he wants the Ingenuity of a Man, he's a Fool to all Rational Intents and Purposes. She then who desires a clear Head must have a pure Heart; and she who has the first in any Measure will never allow her self to be deficient in the other. But you will say what degrees of Purity are requisite in order to Knowledge, and how much must we Know to the end we may heartily endeavour to Purify?

Now in Order to satisfie this demand I consider, That there are certain Notices which we may call the Rudiments of Knowledge, which none who are Rational are without however they came by them. It may happen indeed that a habit of Vice or a long disuse has so obscur'd them that they seem to be extinguish'd, but it does only *seem* so, for were they really extinguish'd the person wou'd be no longer Rational, and no better than the Shade and Picture of a Man. Because as Irrational Creatures act only by the Will of him who made them, and according to the Power of that Mechanisme by which they are form'd, so every one who pretends to Reason, who is a Voluntary Agent and therefore Worthy of Praise or Blame, Reward or Punishment, must *Chuse* his Actions and determine his Will to that Choice by some Reasonings or Principles either true or false, and in proportion to his Principles and the Consequences he deduces from them he is to be accounted, if they are Right and Conclusive a Wise Man, if Evil, Rash and Injudicious a Fool. If then it be the property of Rational Creatures, and Essential to their very Natures to Chuse their Actions, and to determine their Wills to that Choice by such Principles and Reasonings as their Understandings are furnish'd with, they who are desirous to be rank'd in that Order of Beings must conduct their Lives by these Measures, begin with their Intellectuals, inform themselves what are the plain and first Principles of Action and Act accordingly.

By which it appears that there are some degrees of Knowledge necessary before there can be *any* Human Acts, for till we are capable of Chusing our own Actions and directing them by some Principle, tho we Move and Speak and do many such like things, we live not the Life of a Rational Creature but only of an Animal. If it be farther demanded what these Principles are? Not to dispute the Number of 'em here, no body I suppose will deny us one, which is, *That we ought as much as we can to endeavour the Perfecting of our Beings, and that we be as happy as possibly we may.* For this we see is Natural to every Creature of what sort soever, which endeavours to be in as good Condition as its Nature and Circumstances will permit. And now we have got a Principle which one would think were sufficient for the Conduct of our Actions thro the whole Course of our Lives and so indeed it were, cou'd we as easily discern wherein our Happiness consists as 'tis natural to wish and desire it. But herein lies our great mistake and misfortune; for altho we all pursue the same end, yet the means we take to obtain it are Indefinite: There needs no other Proof of this than the looking abroad into the World, which will convince us of the Truth and raise our Wonder at the absurdity, that Creatures of the same Make shou'd take not only so many different, but even contrary Ways to accomplish the same End! We all agree that its fit to be as Happy as we can, and we need no Instructor to teach us this Knowledge, 'tis born with us, and is inseparable from our Being, but we very much need to be Inform'd what is the true Way to Happiness. When the Will comes to ask the Understanding this Question, What must I do to fill up my Vacuities, to accomplish my Nature? Our Reason is at first too weak, and afterwards too often too much sophisticated to return a proper Answer, tho it be the most important concern of our Lives, for according as the Understanding replies to it so is the Moral Conduct of the Will, pure and right if the first be well Inform'd, irregular and vitious if the other be weak and deluded. Indeed our power of Willing exerts it self much sooner than that Rational Faculty which is to Govern It, and therefore 'twill either be left to its own range, or to the Reason of another to direct it; whence it comes that we generally take that Course in our search after Happiness, which Education, Example or Custom puts us in, and, tho not always, yet most commonly, we cast of our first seasoning; which shou'd teach us to take all the care we can that it be Good, and likewise that how Good soever it appear, we be not too much Wedded to and biass'd by it. Well then, the first light of our Understanding must be borrow'd, we must take it on trust till we're furnish'd with a Stock of our own, which we cannot long be without if we do but employ what was lent us in the purifying of our Will, for as this grows more regular the other will enlarge, if it clear up, that will brighten and shine forth with diffusive Rays.

Indeed if we search to the bottom I believe we shall find, that the Corruption of the Heart contributes *more* to the Cloudiness of the Head, than the Clearness of our Light does to the regularity of our Affections, and 'tis oftener seen that our vitious Inclinations keep us Ignorant, than that our Knowledge makes us Good. For it must be confess'd that Purity is not *always* the product of Knowledge; tho the Understanding be appointed by the Author of Nature to direct and Govern the Will, yet many times it's head-strong and Rebellious Subject rushes on precipitately, without its directions. When a Truth comes thwart our Passions, when it dares contradict our mistaken Pleasures and supposed Interests, let the Light shine never so clear we shut our Eyes against it, will not be convinc'd, not because there's any want of Evidence, but because we're *unwilling* to Obey. This is the Rise of all that Infidelity that appears in the world; it is not the Head but the Heart that is the Seat of Atheism. No Man without a brow of Brass, and an Impudence as strong as his Arguments are weak, cou'd demur to the convincing Proofs of Christianity, had not he contracted such diseases in his Passions as make him believe 'tis his Interest to oppose *those* that he may gratify *these*. Yet this is no Objection against what we have been proving, it rather confirms what was said concerning the mutual Relation between the Understanding and the Will, and shews how necessary it is to take care of both, if we wou'd improve and advance either.

Where we must begin. The result of all then, and what gives a satisfactory Answer to the Question where we must begin is this; that some Clearness of Head, some lower degrees of Knowledge, so much at least as will put us an endeavouring after more, is necessary to th' obtaining Purity of Heart. For tho some Persons whom we vulgarly call Ignorant may be honest and Vertuous, yet they are not so in these particulars in which they are Ignorant, but their Integrity in Practising what they know, tho it be but little, causes us to overlook that wherein they Ignorantly transgress. But then any eminent degree of Knowledge, especially of Moral and Divine Knowledge, which is most excellent because most necessary and useful, can never be obtain'd without considerable degrees of Purity: And afterwards when we have procur'd a competent measure of both, they mutually assist each other; the more Pure we are the clearer will our Knowledge be, and the more we Know the more we shall Purify. Accordingly therefore we shall first apply our selves to the Understanding, endeavouring to inform and put it right, and in the next place address to the Will, when we have touch'd upon a few Preliminaries, and endeavoured to remove Obstructions that are prejudicial to both.

CHAP. II.

Containing some Preliminaries. As I. *The removing of Sloth and Stupid Indifferency.* II. *Prejudices arising.* (1.) *From Authority, Education and Custom.* (2.) *From Irregular Self-Love, and Pride. How to cure our Prejudices. Some Remarks upon Change of Opinions, Novelty and the Authority of the Church.* III. *To arm our selves with Courage and Patient Perseverance against* (1.) *The Censures of ill People, and* (2.) *our own Indocility.* IV. *To propose a Right End.*

I. THE first thing I shall advise against is Sloth, and what may be joyn'd with it a stupid Indifference to any thing that is excellent; shall I call it Contentedness with our Condition how low and imperfect soever it be? I will not abuse the Word so much, 'tis rather an ungenerous inglorious Laziness, we doze on in a Circle with our Neighbors, and so we get but Company and Idleness enough, we consider not for what we were made, and what the Condition of our present State requires. And we think our selves good humble Creatures for this, who busy not our Heads with what's out of our Sphere and was never design'd for us, but acquiesce honestly and contentedly in such Employments as the generality of Women have in all Ages been engaged in; for why shou'd we think so well of our selves as to fancy we can be wiser and better than those who have gone before? They went to Heav' no doubt, and we hope that by treading in their steps we likewise in due time may come there, And why should we give our selves any farther trouble? The lowest degree of Bliss in that happy place is more than we deserve, and truly we have too much Humility and Modesty to be Ambitious of a higher.

Thus we hid our faults under the borrowed name of Vertue; an old device taught us by the Enemy of our Souls, and by which he has often deceiv'd us. But 'tis all mistake and nonsense to hope to get to Heaven, if we stint our Endeavours and care for no more but just to get there. For what's at the bottom of this pretended humble temper? No real Love to GOD and longing to enjoy him, no appetite for Heaven, but since we must go thither or to Hell when we quit this dear beloved World, a taking up with that as the more tolerable place. Had we indeed any true Idea of the Life to come, did we but fix our Eyes and Thoughts in the Contemplation of that unconceivable Blessedness, 'twou'd be impossible not to desire it with the warmest vigor, not to be Ambitious of all we are able to attain. For pray wherein do the Joys of Heaven consist, but in the Fruition of GOD the Only and All satisfying Good? and how can we Enjoy Him but by Loving him? And is it not the property of that Passion to think it can never Enjoy enuogh but still to thirst for more? How then can we Love GOD if we do not Long and Labour for the *fullest* Enjoyment of him? And if we do not Love Him how are we like to Enjoy Him in *any* the *least* Degree? He needs neither our Services nor our Company, He loses nothing of His Happiness, tho we will not fit our selves to receive those Communications of it He is desirous t'impart to us; and therefore we've no reason to think He will force His Bliss upon us, render those Faculties He has given us needless, and make us Happy how unfit soever we are for Beatitude. What did we come into the World for? To Eat and to Drink and to pursue the little Impertinencies of this Life? Surely no, our Wise Creator has Nobler Ends whatever we have; He sent us hither to pass our Probation, to Prepare our selves and be Candidates for Eternal Happiness in a better. And how shall this be done but by Labour and Industry? A Labour indeed, but such as carries its Reward with it, besides what it is entituled to hereafter.

The Truth is, that the Condition of our Present State is such, that we can't do *any* thing, much less what's Great and Excellent without some Pain and Weariness of the Flesh; even our very Pleasures are accompanied with Pain, nor wou'd they relish without it, this is the Sauce that recommends them. And why then shall we be averse to the taking a little Pains in that Case only in which 'twill be worth our while? A Title, an Estate, or Place, can neither be got nor kept without some difficulty and trouble; an Amour, can neither be got nor kept without some difficulty and trouble; an Amour, nay even a paltry Dress can't be manag'd without some Thought and Concern, and are our Minds the only thing that do not need, or not deserve them? Has our Bountiful Lord set no limits to our Happiness but the Capacity of our Nature, and shall we set less, and not strive to extend our Capacities to their utmost reach? Has the obliging Son of GOD thought no difficulties too mighty, no Pain too great to undergo for the Love of us, and shall we be so disingenuous and ungrateful as to think a few hours Solitude, a little Meditation and Watchfulness too much to return to his Love? No certainly, we cannot have such narrow groveling hearts; no we are all on Fire, and only want to know wherein to employ our Activity, and how to manage it to the best advantage, which if we wou'd do we must in the next place.

II. Disengage our selves from all our former Prejudices, from our Opinion of Names, Authorities, Customs and the like, not give credit to any thing any longer because we have once believ'd it, but because it carries clear and uncontested Evidence along with it. I shou'd think there needed no more to persuade us to this, than a consideration of the mischiefs these Prejudices do us. These are the grand hindrance in our search after Truth; these dispose us for the reception of Error, and when we have imbib'd confirm us in it; Contract our Souls and shorten our views, hinder the free range of our Thoughts and confine them only to that particular track which these have taken; and in a word, erect a Tyranny over our free born Souls, whilst they suffer nothing to pass for True that has not been stampt at their own Mint. But this is not all their mischief, they are really the root of Scepticism; for when we have taken up an Opinion on weak Grounds and stifly adher'd to it, coming afterwards by some chance or other to be convinc'd of its falseness, the same disposition which induc'd us to receive the Premises without Reason, now inclines us to draw as false a Conclusion from them; and because we seem'd once well assur'd of what now appears to have nothing in't to make us so, therefore we fancy there's nothing certain, that all our Notions are but Probabilities, which stand or fall according to the Ingenuity of their Managers, and so from an unreasonable Obstinacy we pass on to as unreasonable a Levity; so smooth is the transition from believing too easily and too much, to the belief of just nothing at all.

But pray where's the force of this Argument, "This is true because such a Person or such a Number of Men have said it. Or, which commonly weighs more, because I my self, the dear Idol of my own Heart have sometimes embrac'd and perhaps very zealously maintain'd it?" Were we to Poll for Truth, or were our own particular Opinions th'Infallible Standard of it, there were reason to subscribe to the Sentiments of the *Many*, or to be tenacious of our *Own*. But since Truth tho she is bright and ready to reveal her self to all sincere Inquiriers, is not often found by the generality of those who pretend to seek after her, Interest, Applause, or some other little sordid Passion, being really the Mistress they court, whilst she (like Religion in another Case) is made use of for a Stale to carry on the Design the better; since we're commonly too much under the power of Inordinate Affections to have our Understandings always clear and our Judgments certain, are too rash, too precipitate not to need the assistance of a calmer thought, a more serious review; Reason wills that we shou'd think again, and not form our Conclusions or fix our foot till we can honestly say, that we have without Prejudice or Prepossession view'd the matter in Debate on all sides, seen it in every light, have no bias to encline us either way, but are only determin'd by Truth it self, shining brightly in our eyes, and not permitting us to resist the force and Evidence it carries. This I'm sure is what Rational Creatures ought to do, what's then the Reason that they do't not?

Laziness and Idleness in the first place; Thinking is a pain to those who have disus'd it, they will not be at the trouble of carrying on a thought, of pursuing a Meditation till it leads them into the confines of Truth, much less till it puts 'em in possession of her. 'Tis an easier way to follow on in a beaten road, than to launch out into the main Ocean, tho it be in order to the making of new Discoveries; they therefore who would be thought knowing without taking too much pains to be so, suppose 'tis enough to go on in their Fore-fathers steps, to say as they say, and hope they shall get as much Reputation by it as those who have gone before.

Again Self-love, an excellent Principle when true, but the worst and most mischievous when mistaken, disposes us to be retentive of our Prejudices and Errors, especially when it is joyn'd as most commonly it is with Pride and Conceitedness.

The Condition of our present State (as was said before) in which we feel the force of our Passions e're we discern the strength of our Reason, necessitates us to take up with such Principles and Reasonings to direct and determine these Passions as we happen to meet with, tho probably they are far from being just ones, and are such as Education or Accident not right Reason disposes us to; and being inur'd and habituated to these, we at last take them for our own, for parts of our dear beloved selves, and are as unwilling to be divorced from them as we wou'd be to part with a Hand or an Eye or any the most useful Member. Whoever talks contrary to these receiv'd Notions seems to banter us, to persuade us out of our very Senses, and does that which our Pride cannot bear, he supposes we've been all along deceiv'd and must begin anew: We therefore instead of depositing our Old Errors, fish about for Arguments to defend 'em, and do not raise Hypotheses on the Discoveries we have made of Truth, but search for Probabilities to maintain our Hypotheses. And what's the result of all this? Having set out in a wrong way we're resolv'd to persist in it, we stumble in the dark and quarrel with those who wou'd lead us out of it!

But is there no Remedy for this disorder, since we hope that All are not irrecoverably lost, tho too many are so invellop'd in Prejudice that there's little probability of disengaging them? Why really the best that I can think of at present is, to Resolve to be Industrious, and to think no Pains too much to purchase Truth; to consider that our Forefathers were Men of like Passions with us, and are therefore not to be Credited on the score of Authority but of Reason; to remember likewise our own Infirmity, the shortness of our Views, and the bias which our Passion and secular Interests give us; generously to disengage our selves from the deceptions of sense, from all sinister and little Designs, and honestly to search after Truth for no other End but the Glory of GOD, by the accomplishing of our Own and our Neighbours Minds, and when we have humbly implor'd, as now we may very well hope for the Divine Assistance, that the Father of Lights will shine upon us, and that He who is *the Way, the Truth and the Life* will lead us into all Truth; why then we shou'd do well to take notice, That it is of no great consequence to us what our old Opinions are any farther than as we persist in 'em; that there's no necessity that they shou'd be true, but 'tis highly necessary we shou'd fix on what is so; therefore these also must be made to pass the Scrutiny, and be cashier'd if they stand not the test of a severe Examination and sound Reason.

'Tis a great mistake to fancy it a reproach to change our Sentiments, the infamy lies on their side who wilfully and unreasonably adhere to 'em. Not but that it is mean and shameful to be ever on the tip-toe, and indeed to change in any Case where pure and disinteress'd Reason does not oblige us to it. To be once willing to alter our sentiments if there be just occasion for't, wou'd for ever after secure us from Changing, to which the Precipitate and Obstinate are most liable; whereas such as suspend their Judgments till after a sufficient Examination and Weighing of all things they see cause to fix them, do seldom Change, because they can hardly meet with any Reason to do so; and indeed whatever may be the Character of a Wit, Stay'dness and Deliberation is that of a Wise Person.

But as there is an extream on one hand in being too resolutely bent on our Old Opinions, so is there on the other in inordinately thirsting after Novelty. An Opinion is neither better nor worse for being Old or New, the Truth of it is the only thing considerable; tho properly speaking all Truth is Antient, as being from Eternity in the Divine Ideas, 'tis only New in respect of our Discoveries. If we go about to assign a Reason for this insatiable desire of Novelty, I know not how to find a better than our Credulity and easy assent to things inevident. Truth being the proper Object of the Understanding it does naturally search after it, and tho this search will never wholly cease, because our Understandings are more capacious than our Discoveries, and the view of one Truth is but a Preparative to look farther; yet had we clear and certain Evidence for our Conclusions, tho that wou'd not end our Inquiries, it wou'd however satisfie us, so far at least as they had gone. Whereas on the contrary your hunters after Novelty are commonly never satisfied, they pull down today what they had built up yesterday, and Why? But because they concluded too soon? and their Novel Hypothesis is founded on Fancy or Passion, or any thing rather than Right Reason.

But when I speak of the little deference that is to be given to Names, Authorities, and receiv'd Opinions, I extend it no farther than to matters purely Philosophical to mere Humane Truths, and do not design any Prejudice to the Authority of the Church which is of different consideration. For tho it be necessary even in this Case, to deposite whatever may look like a Prejudice, arising from that particular way of Worship, whereby that Communion in which we've been Educated is distinguish'd from all other Christians, yet as to the Substantials of Faith and Practice, tho every one be allow'd to Examine, for they will bear the Test, yet it is not fit that he shou'd draw Conclusions contrary to what has been already determin'd by the Catholick Church, or even by that particular Church of which he is a Member, unless where it does plainly and evidently contradict that sense of Holy Scripture which has been receiv'd by the Church Universal. Nor is this a giving up our selves to Authority barely as such, 'tis only a modest deference to Truth. Philosophical Truths are not open to every Inquirer, an elevated Genius and great application of Mind is requir'd to find them out, nor are they of that importance but that Men may give Scope to their Thoughts, and very often think, tho indeed unreasonably, that they're oblig'd in point of Honour to defend their own Hypotheses. But the Articles of our Faith and the great Principles of Christian Morality are of another Nature, GOD *wou'd have all Men to be sav'd and to come to the Knowlege of* these *Truths,* tho he did not design 'em all for Philosophers, and therefore they carry a Proof and Evidence suited to the very Vulgar, which he who runs may read, which every one ought to acquiesce in, tho according to their leisure and capacity 'tis fit they inquire why. And being a matter of the highest concern such as our Eternal Happiness or Misery depends on, it may reasonably be suppos'd (tho to the shame of our Folly we sometimes find the contrary) that Men won't play fast and loose in a Business of so vast importance, but that all Christians have as they are oblig'd seriously and fully consider'd it, and especially those who are more peculiarly set apart by the Divine Appointment for the study of Sacred Truths. So that to acquiesce in the Authority of the Church, so far as it is here pleaded for is no more than this, The calling in to our assistance the Judgment and Advice of those whom GOD hath set over us, and consequently whom he assists in a more especial manner, to discharge that Function to which he has call'd them; and, in such disputable points as we're not able to determine for our selves, a quiet submission to the Voice of our Guides, whom Modesty will incline us to think have greater Abilities and Assistances, as well as more Time and Opportunity to find out the Truth than we.

As Prejudice fetters the Understanding so does Custom manacle the Will, which scarce knows how to divert from a Track which the generality around it take, and to which it has it self been habituated. It wou'd be too large a digression, to examine throughly a Subject so fit to be consider'd, being it is the root of very much Evil, the last refuge of Vice where it fortifies it self when driven from all other retreats. We shall therefore forbear to enquire from what mistakes it draws its force, what Considerations are proper to disarm it of its power, and what else might be of use to deliver us from its Slavery, and only remark; That tho great deference is to be paid to the Ways and Usages of the Wise and Good, yet considering that these are the least number of Mankind, 'tis the Croud who will make the Mode, and consequently it will be as absurd as they are: Therefore Custom cannot Authorise a Practice if Reason Condemns it, the following a Multitude is no excuse for the doing of Evil. None but the Weak and Inconsiderable swim down with the Torrent, brave Spirits delight to stem the Tide, they know no Conquest so Glorious, because none so difficult, as that which is obtain'd over foolish and ill-grounded Maxims and sinful Customs; What wou'd they not do to restore Mankind to their Lawful Liberty, and to pull down this worst of Tyrannies, because it enslaves the very Souls of Men?

III. But a Generous Resolution and Courageous Industry are not only necessary to enable us to throw off Sloth and to Conquer the Prejudices of Education, Authority and Custom, the same Resolution and Courage which help'd us to this Victory, must secure and continue to us the Fruits of it. We shall have need of Patience and constant Perseverance thro the whole course of our Lives if we mean to prosecute the noble Design we have begun; we must not think the Business is over when we have smooth'd the entrance; there will still be Difficulties, tho no insuperable ones, but such as will wear off by degrees, the greatest uneasiness being in the first effort. And tho our Progress shou'd not happen to be answerable to our Desires, there's no reason to be discourag'd, we shou'd rather be animated by such noble Desires to greater Industry. Where's the Glory of an easy Victory? 'Tis Labour and Cost that inhanses the value of every thing. And to the end we may not be discourag'd, 'tis fit that we arm our selves against all Accidents by considering them before hand. We have the Malice and Industry of many Cunning and Powerful Adversaries, as well as our own indocility to contend with. The grand Enemy of Mankind is very unwilling that they shou'd arrive at that State of Innocence and Perfection from which he fell, and of all the Artifices he makes use of to hinder it, scarce any's more effectual than the mischief he excites us to do one another. What are they employ'd in but his Service who will neither do any thing that's excellent themselves, nor if they could hinder, suffer it to be done by others? Who employ all their little Wit and Pains in Scoffing at such who they say in derision wou'd be wiser then their Neighbours? We must be content to suffer a scornful sneer, a parcel of hard Names and a little ridiculing, if we're Resolv'd to do such things as do not deserve 'em. Dogs will bark at the Moon, and perhaps for no other reason but because she is out of their reach, elevated above them. But the Author of our Nature to whom all the Inconveniencies we are liable to in this Earthy Pilgrimage are fully known, has endow'd us with Principles sufficient to carry us safely thro them all, if we will but observe and make use of 'em. One of these is *Generosity*, which (so long as we keep it from degenerating into Pride) is of admirable advantage to us in this matter. It was not fit that Creatures capable of and made for Society, shou'd be wholly Independent, or Indifferent to each others Esteem and Commendation; nor was it convenient considering how seldom these are justly distributed, that they shou'd too much regard and depend on them. It was requisite therefore that a desire of our Neighbours Good Opinion shou'd be implanted in our Natures to the end we might be excited to do such things as deserve it, and yet withall a Generous neglect of it, if they unjustly withheld it where it was due. There's so little reason that we shou'd be discourag'd from what is truly excellent and becoming on account of being Scoft and Laugh'd at for it, that on the contrary this is a new accession to our Glory, we never shine so Illustriously as when we break thro these little Clouds and Oppositions which impotently attempted to obscure our Rays. To be Reproach'd for Weldoing is a higher Encomium, than the loftiest Praises when we do not deserve them: So that let the World think as it list, whilst we are in the pursuit of true Wisdom, our Reputation is secur'd, our Crown is furbishing, and tho it do not shine out in this Envious and Ill-natur'd World, it will however, which is infinitely more desirable appear in all its Lustre and Splendor in a better.

And as we disregard the Censures of ill People, so are we patiently to bear with our own backwardness and indocility. There goes a good deal of Time and Pains, of Thought and Watchfulness to the rooting out of Ill-habits, to the fortifying our Minds against foolish Customs, and to the making that easie and pleasant which us'd to be irksome to us. But we ought not to be disheartn'd, since 'tis necessary to be done, and we cannot reasonably say 'tis Impossible, till we've attempted and fail'd in't. But then let's attempt it in the most prudent Method, use the properest Means, allow sufficient Time for their Operation and to make the essay: Let's not set about it by fits, or in one or two good Moods, nor expect it will be done on a sudden, but by degrees and in a proper season, making it our main Design and Business, and then I dare confidently affirm the success will answer the Pains we have spent about it.

IV. But one thing more, and then I shall go on as well I can, to lay down what seems to me the best Method for Improvement. Whoever wou'd Act to purpose must propose some End to themselves, and keep it still in their Eye thro'out their whole progress. Life without this is a disproportionate unseemly thing, a confused huddle of broken, contradictory Actions, such as afford us nothing but the being asham'd of 'em. But do we need to be taught our End? One wou'd rather think there were no occasion to mention it, did not Experience daily convince us how many there are who neglect it. What End can Creatures have but their Creators Glory? And did they truly understand their own Happiness 'tis certain they wou'd have no other, since this is the only way of procuring their own Felicity. But it is not enough to have barely an implicit and languid desire of it, 'twere much better to hold it ever in view, and that all our Actions had in their proportion a warm and immediate tendency thither. This wou'd stamp the impression of Holiness upon the most indifferent Action, and without this what is Materially and to all outward appearance very good, is really and truly no better than a specious folly. We are not made for our selves, nor was it ever design'd we shou'd be ador'd and idolized by one another. Our Faculties were given us for Use not Ostentation, not to make a noise in the World, but to be serviceable in it, to declare the Wisdom, Power and Goodness, of that All-Perfect Being from whom we derive *All* our Excellencies, and in whose Service they ought *Wholly* to be employ'd. Did our Knowlege serve no other purpose than the exalting us in our own Opinion, or in that of our Fellow Creatures, the furnishing us with Materials for a quaint Discourse, an agreeable Conversation, 'twere scarce worth while to be at the trouble of attaining it. But when it enlarges the Capacity of our Minds, gives us nobler Ideas of the Majesty, the Grandeur and Glorious Attributes of our adorable Creator, Regulates our Wills and makes us more capable of Imitating and Enjoying him, 'tis then a truly sublime thing, a worthy Object of our Industry: And she who does not make this the End of her Study, spends her Time and Pains to no purpose or to an ill one.

We have no better way of finding out the true End of any thing, than by observing to what Use it is most adapted. Now the Art of *Well-Living*, the Study of the Divine Will and Law, that so we may be Conformable to it in all things, is what we're peculiarly fitted for and destin'd to, what ever has not such a Tendency, either Directly or at least Remotely, is besides the purpose. Rational Studies therefore next to GOD's Word bid fairest for our Choice, because they best answer the Design above mention'd. Truths merely Speculative and which have no influence upon Practice, which neither contribute to the good of Soul or Body, are but idle Amusements, an impertinent and criminal waste of Time. To be able to speak many Languages, to give an Historical Account of all Ages, Opinions and Authors, to make a florid Harangue, or defend right or wrong the Argument I've undertaken, may give me higher thoughts of my Self but not of GOD, this is the *Knowlege that pufeth up*, in the Words of the Apostle, and seldom leads us to that *Charity which Edifieth*.

And as the Understanding so the Will must be duly directed to its End and Object. Morality is so consonant to the Nature of Man, so adapted to his Happiness, that had not his Under-

76

standing been darkn'd by the Fall, and his whole Frame disorder'd and weakned, he wou'd Naturally have practis'd it. And according as he recovers himself, and casts off those Clouds which Eclipse his Reason, so proportionably are his Actions more agreeable to Moral Precepts, and tho we suppose him ignorant of any higher end, he will however do such things as they enjoyn him, to th'intent he may be easy, obtain a good Reputation, and enjoy himself and this World the better. Now were we sure that Reason wou'd always maintain its ground against Passion and Appetite, such an one might be allow'd to be a good Neighbour, a Just Ruler, a plausible Friend or the like, and wou'd well enough discharge the Relative Duties of Society, and do nothing misbecoming the dignity of Human Nature. But considering how weak our Reason is, how unable to maintain its Authority and oppose the incursions of sense, without the assitance of an inward and Spiritual Sensation to strengthen it, 'tis highly necessary that we use due endeavours to procure a lively relish of our true Good, a Sentiment that will not only Ballance, but if attended to and improv'd, very much out-weigh the Pleasures of our Animal Nature. Now this is no otherwise to be obtain'd than by directing the Will in an elicit Act to GOD as its only Good, so that the sole End of all its movements, may be to draw near, to acquiesce in and be united to him. For as all Natural Motions are easie and pleasant, so this being the only Natural Motion of the Will must needs be unspeakably delightful to it. Besides that peculiar delectation, which this Fountain of Joy bestows as a Donative, on all who thus sincerly address themselves to him. So that it is not enough to be Morally Good because 'tis most Reputable and Easie, and most for our Pleasure and Interest in the present World, as this will never secure our Duty, so is it too low an End for a Creature capable of Immortality to propose, nothing less than an intire devoting of our selves to the End for which we were made, the Service and Enjoyment of the most amiable and only Good, can keep us Constantly and Uniformly in our Duty, or is a Design that 's worthy of us.

CHAP. III.

Concerning the Improvement of the Understanding. I. Of the Capacity of the Humane Mind in General. II. Of Particular Capacities. III. The most common Infirmities incident to the Understanding and their Cure. IV. A Natural Logic, And V. Rhetoric propos'd. VI. The Application and Use of our Knowlege.

THE perfection of the Understanding consisting in the Clearness and Largeness of its view, it improves proportionably as its Ideas become Clearer and more Extensive. But this is not so to be understood as if all sorts of Notices contributed to our Improvement, there are some things which make us no wiser when we know 'em, others which 'tis best to be ignorant of. But that Understanding seems to me the most exalted, which has the Clearest and most Extensive view of such Truths as are suitable to its Capacity, and Necessary or Convenient to be Known in this Present State. For being that we are but Creatures, our Understanding in its greatest Perfection has only a limited excellency. It has indeed a vast extent, and it were not amiss if we tarried a little in the Contemplation of its Powers and Capacities, provided that the Prospect did not make us giddy, that we remember from whom we have receiv'd them, and ballance those lofty Thoughts which a view of our Intellectuals may occasion, with the depressing ones which the irregularity of our Morals will suggest, and that we learn from this inspection, how indecorous it is to busy this bright side of us in mean things, seeing it is capable of such noble ones.

Human Nature is indeed a wonderful Composure admirable in its outward structure, but much more excellent in the Beauties of its Inward, and she who considers in whose Image her Soul was Created, and whose Blood was shed to Redeem it, cannot prize it too much, nor forget to pay it her utmost regard. There's nothing in this Material World to be compar'd to't, all the gay things we dote on, and for which we many times expose our Souls to ruin, are of no consideration in respect of it. They are not the good of the Soul, it's happiness depends not on 'em, but they often deceive and withdraw it from its true Good. It was made for the Contemplation and Enjoyment of its GOD, and all Souls are capable of this tho in a different degree and by measures somewhat different, as we hope will appear from that which follows.

I. Truth in general is the Object of the Understanding, but all Truths are not equally Evident, because of the Limitation of the Humane Mind, which tho' it can gradually take in many Truths, yet cannot any more than our sight attend to many things at once: And likewise, because GOD has not thought fit to communicate such Ideas to us as are necessary to the disquisition of some particular Truths. For knowing nothing without us but by the Idea we have of it, and Judging only according to the Relation we find between two or more Ideas, when we cannot discover the Truth we search after by Intuition or the immediate comparison of two Ideas, 'tis necessary that we shou'd have a third by which to compare them. But if this middle Idea be wanting, though we have sucient Evidence of those two which we wou'd compare, because we have a Clear and Distinct Conception of them, yet we are Ignorant of those Truths which wou'd arise from their Comparison, because we want a third by which to compare them.

To give an instance of this in a point of great consequence, and of late very much controverted tho to little purpose, because we take a wrong method, and wou'd make that the Object of Science which is properly the Object of Faith, the Doctrine of the Trinity. Revelation which is but an exaltation and improvement of Reason has told us, That the Father is GOD, the Son is GOD, and the Holy Ghost is GOD, and our Idea of the Godhead of any one of these Persons, is as clear as our Idea of any of the other. Both Reason and Revelation assure us that GOD is One Simple Essence, Undivided, and Infinite in all Perfection, this is the Natural Idea which we have of GOD. How then can the Father be GOD, the Son GOD, and the Holy Ghost GOD, when yet there is but One GOD? That these two Propositions are true we are certain, both because GOD who cannot lie has Reveal'd 'em, and because we have as clear an Idea of 'em as it is possible a Finite Mind shou'd have of an Infinite Nature. But we cannot find out how this should be, by the bare Comparison of these two Ideas without the help of a third by which to compare them. This GOD has not thought fit to impart to us, the Prospect it wou'd have given us wou'd have been too dazling, too bright for Mortality to bear, and we ought to acquiesce in the Divine Will. So then, we are well assur'd that these two Propositions are true, *There is but one GOD;* And, *There are three Persons in the Godhead:* but we know not the *Manner* how these things are. Nor can our acquiescence be thought Unreasonable, nor the Doctrine we subscribe to be run down as absurd and contradictory by every little warm Disputer and Pretender to Reason, whose Life is perhaps a continual contradiction to it, and he knows little of it besides the Name. For we ought not to think it strange that GOD has folded up his own Nature, not in Darkness, but in an adorable and inaccessible Light, since his Wisdom sees it fit to keep us ignorant of our own. We know and feel the Union between our Soul and Body, but who amongst us sees so clearly, as to find out with Certitude and Exactness, the secret ties which unite two such different Substances, or how they are able to act upon each other? We are conscious of our own Liberty, who ever denies it, denies that he is capable of Rewards and Punishments, degrades his Nature and makes himself but a more curious piece of Mechanism; and none but Atheists will call in question the Providence of GOD, or deny that he Governs *All,* even the most Free of all his Creatures. But who can reconcile me these? Or adjust the limits between GOD's Prescience and Mans Free-will? Our Understandings are sufficiently illuminated to lead us to the Fountain of Life and Light, we do or may know enough to fill our Souls with the noblest Conceptions, the humblest Adoration, and the intirest Love of the Author of our Being, and what can we desire farther? If we make so ill a Use of that Knowledge which we have, as to be so far puffed up with it, as to turn it against him who gave it, how dangerous would it be for us to have more Knowledge, in a State in which we have so little Humility! But if vain Man will pretend to Wisdom, let him first learn to know the length of his own line.

Tho the Human Intellect has a large extent, yet being limited as we have already said, this Limitation is the Cause of those different Modes of Thinking, which for distinction sake we call Faith, Science and Opinion. For in this present and imperfect State in which we know not any thing by Intuition, or immediate View, except a few first Principles which we call Self-evident, the most of our Knowlege is acquir'd by Reasoning and Deduction: And these three Modes of Understanding, Faith, Science and Opinion are no otherwise distinguish'd than by the different degrees of Clearness and Evidence in the Premises from whence the Conclusion is drawn.

Knowlege in a proper and restricted Sense and as appropriated to Science, signifies that clear Perception which is follow'd by a firm assent to Conclusions rightly drawn from Premises of which we have clear and distinct Ideas. Which Premises or Principles must be so clear and Evident, that supposing us reasonable Creatures, and free from Prejudices and Passions, (which for the time they predominate as good as deprive us of our Reason) we cannot withhold our assent from them without manifest violence to our Reason.

But if the Nature of the thing be such as that it admits of no undoubted Premises to argue from, or at least we don't at present know of any, or that the Conclusion does not so necessarily follow as to give a perfect satisfaction to the Mind and to free it from all hesitation, that which we think of it is then call'd Opinion.

Again, If the Medium we make use of to prove the Proposition be Authority, the Conclusion which we draw from it is said to be Believ'd; This is what we call Faith, and when the Authority is GOD's a Divine Faith.

Moral Certainty is a Species of Knowlege whose Proofs are of a compounded Nature, in part resembling those which belong to Science, and partly those of Faith. We do not make the whole Process our selves, but depend on another for the *immediate* Proof, but we our selves deduce the *Mediate* from Circumstances and Principles as Certain and almost as Evident as those of Science, and which lead us to the immediate Proofs and make it unreasonable to doubt of 'em. Indeed we not seldom deceive our selves in this manner, by inclining alternately to both extre..es. ˆ ˜etimes we reject Truths which are Morally Certain as Conjectural and Probable only, because they have not a Physical and Mathematical Certainty, which they are incapable of. At another time we embrace the slightest Conjectures and any thing that looks with Probability, as moral Certainties and real Verities, if Fancy, Passion or Interest recommend them; so ready are we to be determin'd by these rather than by solid Reason.

In this enumeration of the several ways of Knowing, I have not reckon'd the Senses, in regard that we're more properly said to be *Conscious* of than to *Know* such things as we perceive by Sensation. And also because that Light which we suppose to be let into our Ideas by our Senses is indeed very dim and fallacious, and not to be relied on till it has past the Test of Reason; neither do I think there's any Mode of Knowledge which mayn't be reduc'd to those already mentioned.

Now tho there's a great difference between Opinion and Science, true Science being immutable but Opinion variable and uncertain, yet there is not such a difference between Faith and Science as is usually suppos'd. The difference consists not in the Certainty but in the way of Proof; the Objects of Faith are as Rationally and as Firmly Prov'd as the Objects of Science, tho by another way. As Science Demonstrates things that are *Seen*, so Faith is the Evidence of such as are *Not Seen*. And he who rejects the Evidence of Faith in such things as belong to its Cognizance, is as unreasonable as he who denies Propositions in Geometry that are prov'd with Mathematical exactness.

There's nothing true which is not in it self demonstrable, or which we should not pronounce to be true had we a Clear and Intuitive View of it. But as was said above we see very few things by Intuition, neither are we furnish'd with Mediums to make the Process our selves in Demonstrating all Truths, and therefore there are some Truths which we must either be totally ignorant of, or else receive them on the Testimony of another Person, to whose Understanding they are clear and manifest tho not to ours. And if this Person be one who can neither be Deceiv'd nor Deceive, we're as certain of those Conclusions which we prove by his Authority, as we're of those we demonstrate by our own Reason: nay more Certain, by how much his Reason is more Comprehensive and Infallible than our own.

Science is the following the Process our Selves upon Clear

and Evident Principles; Faith is a Dependance on the Credit of another, in such matters as are out of our View. And when we have very good Reason to submit to the Testimony of the Person we Believe, Faith is as Firm, and those Truths it discovers to us as truly Intelligible, and as strongly Prov'd in their kind as Science.

In a word, as every Sense so every Capacity of the Understanding has its proper Object. The Objects of Science are things within our View, of which we may have Clear and Distinct Ideas, and nothing shou'd be determin'd here without Clearness and Evidence. To be able to repeat any Persons *Dogma* without forming a Distinct Idea of it our selves, is not to Know but to Remember; and to have a Confused Indeterminate Idea is to Conjecture not to Understand.

The Objects of Faith are as Certain and as truly, Intelligible in themselves as those of Science, as has been said already, only we become persuaded of the Truth of them by another Method, we do not *See* them so clearly and distinctly as to be unable to disbelieve them. Faith has a mixture of the Will that it may be rewardable, for who will thank us for giving our Assent where it was impossible to withold it? Faith then may be said to be a sort of Knowlege capable of Reward, and Men are Infidels not for want of Conviction, but thro an *Unwillingness* to Believe.

But as it is a fault to Believe in matters of Science, where we may expect Demonstration and Evidence, so it is a reproach to our Understanding and a proof of our Disingenuity, to require that sort of Process peculiar to Science, for the Confirmation of such Truths as are not the proper Objects of it. It is as ridiculous as to reject Musick, because we cannot Tast or Smell it, or to deny there is such a thing as Beauty because we do not hear it. He who wou'd See with his Ears and Hear with his Eyes may indeed set up in *Bedlam* for a Man of an extraordinary reach, a Sagacious Person who won't be impos'd on, one who must have more Authentick proofs than his dull Fore-fathers were content with. But Men of dry Reason and a moderate Genius, I suppose will think Nature has done very well in allotting to each Sense its proper employment, and such as these will as readily acknowlege that it is as Honourable for the Soul to Believe what is truly the Object of Faith, as it is for her to Know what is really the Object of her Knowlege. And were we not strangely perverse we shou'd not scruple Divine Authority when we daily submit to Human. Whoever has not seen *Paris* has nothing but Human Authority to assure him there is such a place, and yet he wou'd be laugh'd at as ridiculous who shou'd call it in question, tho he may as well in this as in another Case pretend that his Informers have designs to serve, intend to impose on him and mock his Credulity. Nay how many of us daily make that a matter of Faith which indeed belongs to Science, by adhering blindly to the Dictates of some famous Philosopher in Physical Truths, the Principles of which we have as much right to examine, and to make deductions from 'em as he had?

To sum up all: We may know enough for all the purposes of Life, enough to busie this active Faculty of Thinking, to employ and entertain the spare Intervals of Time and to keep us from Rust and Idleness, but we must not pretend to fathom all Depths with our short Line, we shou'd be Wise unto Sobriety, and reckon that we know very little if we go about to make our *Own* Reason the Standard of all Truth. It is very certain that nothing is True but what is conformable to Reason, that is to the Divine Reason of which ours is but a short faint Ray, and it is as certain that there are many Truths which Human Reason cannot Comprehend. Therefore to be throughly sensible of the Capacity of the Mind, to discern precisely its Bounds and Limits and to direct our Studies and Inquiries accordingly, to Know what is to be Known, and to Believe what is to be Believ'd is the property of a Wise Person. To be content with too little Knowlege, or to aspire to over-much is equally a fault, to make that use of our Understandings which GOD has Fitted and Design'd them for is the Medium which we ought to take. For the difference between a Plow-man and a Doctor does not seem to me to consist in this, That the Business of the one is to search after Knowlege, and that the other has nothing to do with it. No, whoever has a Rational Soul ought surely to employ it about some Truth or other, to procure for it right Ideas, that its Judgments may be true tho its Knowlege be not very extensive. But herein lies the difference, that tho Truth is the Object of every Individual Understanding, yet all are not equally enlarg'd nor able to comprehend so much; and they whose Capacities and Circumstances of Living do not fit 'em for it, lie not

84

under that obligation of extending their view which Persons of a larger reach and greater leisure do. There is indeed often times a mistake in this matter, People who are not fit will be puzling their heads to little purpose, and those who are prove Slothful and decline the trouble; and thus it will be if we do not throughly understand our selves, but suffer Pride or Ease to make the estimate.

II. It is therefore very fit that after we have consider'd the Capacity of the Understanding in general, we shou'd descend to the view of our own particular, observing the bent and turn of our own Minds, which way our Genius lies and to what it is most inclin'd. I see no reason why there may not be as great a variety in Minds as there is in Faces, that the Soul as well as the Body may not have something in it to distinguish it, not only from all other Intelligent Natures but even from those of its own kind. There are different proportions in Faces which recommend them to some Eyes sooner than to others, and tho *All* Truth is amiable to a Reasonable Mind, and proper to employ it, yet why may there not be some particular Truths, more agreeable to each individual Understanding than others are? Variety gives Beauty to the Material World and why not to the Intellectual? We can discern the different Abilities which the Wise Author of all things has endow'd us with, the different Circumstances in which he has plac'd us in reference to this World and the Concerns of an Animal Life, that so we may be mutually useful, and that since each single Person is too limited and confin'd to attend to many, much less to all things, we may receive from each other a reciprocal advantage, and why may we not think he has done the like in respect of Truth? that since it is too much for one, our united Strength shou'd be employ'd in the search of her. Especially since the Divine Being who contains in himself all Reality and Truth is Infinite in Perfection, and therefore shou'd be Infinitely Ador'd and Lov'd; and If Creatures are by their being so uncapable of rendering to their Incomprehensible Creator an Adoration and Love that's worthy of him, it is but decorous that they shou'd however do as much as they can. All that variety of sublime Truths of Beautiful and Wondrous Objects which surround us, are nothing else but a various display of his unbounded Excellencies, and why shou'd any of 'em pass unobserv'd? Why shou'd not every individual Understanding be in a more especial manner fitted for and employ'd in the disquisition of some particular Truth and Beauty? 'Tis true after all our researches we can no more sufficiently Know GOD than we can worthily Love him, and are as much unable to find out all his Works as we are his Nature, yet this shou'd only prompt us to exert *All* our Powers and to do our best, since even *that* were too little cou'd we possibly do more. We can never offer to him so much Praise as he deserves, and therefore it is but fit that he shou'd have *All* that Mankind can possibly render him. He is indeed immutable in his own Nature, but those discoveries we daily make of his Operations will always afford us somewhat New and Surprizing, for this All-glorious Sun the Author of Life and Light is as inexhaustible a Source of Truth as he is of Joy and Happiness.

If then we are convinc'd that there's some peculiar Task allotted us, our next business will be to enquire what it is. To know our own Strength and neither to over nor underrate our selves is one of the most material points of Wisdom, and which indeed we are most commonly ignorant of, else we shou'd not reach at all, how unable soever we are to attain it, nor make so many successless attempts and be forc'd to come off with that pitiful Apology, *I was mistaken, I did not think it.* But we can scarce duly estimate our Understandings till we have regulated our Wills, reform'd Self-love and a train of immortified Passions, which it is not our Business to speak of here, we shall have occasion to do't hereafter. Let it suffice that we remark a frequent Error which these engage us in, that is, an aptness to lessen the Human Mind, to detract from its Grandeur and abridge its Powers when we consider it in General, and as great a forwardness when we look on our selves to extend our Abilities beyond their bounds. Are we conscious of a Defect? the shallowness of Human Reason at large must bear the blame, we Harangue very excellently on the Ignorance and Vanity of Mankind, and it were well if we rested there, and wou'd forbear to murmur even at our Creator himself for allowing us so scanty a Portion. But if Reason has shone out, dispelling those Clouds which Eclips'd the bright face of Truth, we arrogate all to our selves. *My* Discovery, *My* Hypothesis, the Strength and Clearness of *My* Reasonings, rather than the Truth are what we wou'd expose to view; 'tis that we Idolize our selves and wou'd have every one Admire and Celebrate. And yet all this is no more perhaps than another has done before us, or at least might have done with our Opportunities and Advantages. The reverse of this procedure wou'd become us better, and it were more Glorious as well as more Just to ascribe the Excellencies of the Mind to Human Nature in the Lump and to take the Weaknesses to our selves. By this we shou'd both avoid Sloth, (the best use we can make of our Ignorance and Infirmity being first to be humbled for, and then sedulously to endeavour their Amendment) and likewise secure our Industry from the Mixtures of Pride and Envy. By looking on our own Acquisitions as a general Treasure, in which the Whole have a Right, we shou'd pretend to no more than a share; and considering our selves as Parts of the same Whole, we should expect to find our own account in th' Improvement of every part of it, which wou'd restrain us from being puft up with the Contemplation of our Own, and from repining at our Neighbours Excellencies. For let Reason shine forth where it may, as we can't engross, so neither can we be excluded from sharing in the Benefit, unless we willfully exclude our selves; everyone being the better for True Worth and Good Sense, except the little Soul'd Enviers of 'em.

To help us to the Knowledge of our own Capacities the Informations of our Friends, nay even of our Enemies may be useful. The former if Wise and True will direct us to the same Course to which our Genius Points, and the latter will industriously endeavour to divert us from it, and we can't be too careful that these don't disguise themselves under the specious appearance of the former, to do us an ill-turn the more effectually. For it is not seldom seen that such as pretend great Concern for us, will press us on to such Studies or Ways of Living as inwardly they know we are unfit for, thereby to gratify their Secret Envy, by diverting us from that to which our Genius disposes, and in which therefore they have reason to suppose we wou'd be Excellent. But tho we may make use of the Opinions of both, yet if we will be Sincere and Ingenuous we cannot have a more faithful Director than our own heart. He who gave us these Dispositions will excite us to the Use and Improvement of 'em; and unless we drive him from us by our Impurity, or thro negligence and want of Attention let slip his secret Whispers, this Master within us will lay most in our view such Lessons as he wou'd have us take. Our care then must be to open our Eyes to that Beam of Light which does in a more especial manner break in upon us, to fix them steadily, and to examine accurately those notices which are most vividly represented to us, and to lay out our Thoughts and Time in the Cultivation of 'em. It may be our Humor won't be gratified, nor our Interest serv'd by such a Method. Other Business or Amusements put on a finer Garb, and come attended with more Charms and Grandeur, these recommend us to the World, make us Belov'd and Illustrious in it: Whilst the followers of Truth are despis'd and look'd askew on, as fantastick Speculatists, unsociable Thinkers, who pretend to see farther than their Neighbours, to rectifie what Custom has establish'd, and are so Unmannerly as to Think and Talk out of the Common way. He who speaks Truth makes a Satyr on the greatest part of Mankind, and they are not over apt to forgive him, he contradicts the vogue of the Times, is so hardy as to lay open Men's darling Errors, to draw a lively Picture of their most secret Corruptions, a Representation which they cannot bear. Their Gall is touch'd proportionably as their Wounds are more deeply search'd into, altho it be only in order to a Cure. They therefore who Love Truth shall be Hated by the Most, who tho they openly pretend to Honour, yet secretly Malign her, because she reproaches them. And as a plausible Life is not often a very Religious one, which made the best Judge pronounce a Woe on those whom all Men shall speak well of, so neither is the most Just and Illuminated Understanding the most admir'd and trusted to, but a plausible Speaker, as well as a plausible Liver, commonly bears away the Bell. If then we consult our Passions and Vanity we shall go near to determine amiss, and make that use of our Intellectuals which Fancy or Interest pushes us on to, not which Nature has fitted us for. Hence it is that those who might have done very well in some Studies and Employments, make but bungling work when they apply themselves to others. We go on apace when the Wind and Tide are on our side, but it costs us much Labour, and we make little speed, when we Row against both.

And as a due Consideration of our Particular Capacity wou'd put us right in our own Studies so wou'd it keep us from clashing with our Neighbours, whom we many times Contend with not so much out of a Love to Truth, as thro a humor of Contradiction, or because we think this the best way to shew our Parts, and by this tryal of Skill to exalt our selves above them. But is there no better way to discover our Penetration, and to try our Strength, than by a Malicious and Litigious Opposition? The field of Truth is large, and after all the Discoveries that have been made by those who have gone before, there will still be untroden Paths, which they who have the Courage and Skill may beat out and beautify. If then instead of Jostling and Disputing with our Fellow Travellers, of bending all the force of our Wit to Contradict and Oppose those advances which they make, we wou'd well understand, duly Employ and kindly Communicate our Peculiar Talent, how much more Service might we do our Lord, how much more useful might we be to one another? What vast Discoveries wou'd be made in the wide Ocean of Truth? How many Moral Irregularities wou'd be observ'd and rectify'd? We shoul'd be restrain'd from aspiring to things above our reach, move regularly in our own Sphere, not abuse those good Parts which were given us for Common Benefit, to the Destruction of our selves and others, be in a fair way to discern the Defects of our Mind and to proceed to the Cure of 'em.

III. We have already exprest our thoughts concerning the Capacity and Perfection of the Understanding, and what has been said if duly consider'd, is sufficient to bring every particular Person acquainted with their own defects. But because they who need Amendment most, are commonly least dispos'd to make such reflections as are necessary to procure it, we will spend a few Pages in considering for them, and in observing the most usual defects of the Thinking Faculty.

If we are of their Opinion who say that the Understanding is only Passive, and that Judgment belongs to the Will, I see not any Defect the former can have, besides Narrowness and a disability to extend it self to many things, which is indeed incident to all Creatures, the brightest Intelligence in the highest Order of Angels is thus defective, as well as the meanest Mortal, tho in a less degree. Nor ought it to be complain'd of, since 'tis Natural and Necessary, we may as well desire to be Gods as desire to Know all things. Some sort of Ignorance therefore, or

Non perception we cannot help; a Finite Mind, suppose it as large as you please, can never extend it self to Infinite Truths. But no doubt it is in our Power to remedy a great deal more than we do, and probably a larger Range is allowed us than the most Active and Enlightned Understanding has hitherto reach'd. Ignorance then can't be avoided but Error may, we cannot Judge of things of which we have no Idea, but we can suspend our Judgment about those of which we have, till clearness and evidence oblige us to pass it. Indeed in strictness of Speech the Will and not the Understanding is blameable when we Think amiss, since the latter opposes not the Ends for which GOD made it, but readily extends it self as far as it can, receiving such Impressions as are made on it; 'tis the former that directs it to such Objects, that fills up its Capacity with such Ideas as are foreign to its Business and of no use to it, or which does not at least oppose the incursions of Material things, and deface as much as it is able those impressions which Sensible Objects leave in the Imagination. But since it is not material to the present Design, whether Judgment belongs to the Understanding or Will, we shall not nicely distinguish how each of 'em is employ'd in acquiring Knowledge, but treat of 'em both together in this Chapter, allotted to the Service of the Studious, who when they are put in the way may by their own Meditations and Experience, rectifie the mistakes and supply the Omissions we happen to be guilty of.

They who apply themselves to the Contemplation of Truth, will perhaps at first find a Contraction or Emptiness of Thought, and that their Mind offers nothing on the Subject they wou'd consider, is not ready at unfolding, nor in representing correspondent Ideas to be compar'd with it, is as it were asleep or in a Dream, and tho' not empty of all Thought, yet Thinks nothing clearly or to the purpose. The Primary Cause of this is that Limitation which all Created Minds are Subject to, which Limitation appears more visible in some than in others, either because some Minds are endow'd by their Creator with a larger Capacity than the rest, or if you are not inclin'd to think so, then by reason of the Indisposition of the Bodily Organs, which cramps and contracts the Operations of the Mind. And that Person whose Capacity of receiving Ideas is very little, whose Ideas are disorder'd, and not capable of being so dispos'd as that they may be compar'd in order to the forming of a Judgment, is a Fool or little better. If we find this to be our Case, and that after frequent tryals there appears no hopes of Amendment, 'tis best to desist, we shall but lose our Labour, we may do some Good in an Active Life and Employments that depend on the Body, but we're altogether unfit for Contemplation and the Exercises of the Mind. Yet e'er we give out let's see if it be thus with us in all Cases: Can we Think and Argue Rationally about a Dress, an Intreague, an Estate? Why then not upon better Subjects? The way of Considering and Meditating justly is the same on all Occasions. 'Tis true, there will fewest Ideas arise when we wou'd Meditate on such Subjects as we've been least conversant about; but this is a fault which it is in our power to remedy, first by Reading or Discoursing, and then by frequent and serious Meditation, of which hereafter.

As those we have been speaking of are hindred in their search after Truth, thro a want of Ideas out of which to deduce it, so there are another sort who are not happy in their Enquiries, on account of the multiude and Impetuosity of theirs. Volatileness of Thought, very pernicious to true Science, is a fault which People of warm Imaginations and Active Spirits are apt to fall into. Such a Temper is readily dispos'd to receive Errors and very well qualified to propagate them, especially if a volubility of Speech be join'd to it. These thro an immoderate nimbleness of Thinking skip from one Idea to another, without observing due Order and Connexion, they content themselves with a superficial view, a random glance, and depending on the vigor of their Imagination, are took with Appearances, never tarrying to penetrate the Subject, or to find out Truth if she float not upon the Surface. A multitude of Ideas not relating to the matter they design to think of rush in upon them, and their easie Mind entertains all comers how impertinent soever; instead of examining the Question in debate they are got into the Clouds, numbring the Cities in the Moon and building Airy Castles there. Nor is it easie to cure this Defect, since it deceives others as well as those who have it with a shew of very great Ingenuity. The vivacity of such Persons makes their Conversation plausible, and taking with those who consider not much, tho not with the Judicious; it procures for them the Character of Wit, but hinders them from being Wise. For truth is not often found by such as won't take Time to examine her Counterfeits, to distinguish between Evidence and Probability, Realities and Appearances, but who thro a conceit of their own sharp-sightedness think they can pierce to the bottom with the first glance.

To cure this Distemper perfectly perhaps it will be necessary to apply to the Body as well as to the Mind: The Animal Spirits must be lessen'd, or rendred more Calm and Manageable; at least they must not be unnaturally and violently mov'd, by such a Diet, or such Passions, Designs and Divertisments as are likely to put 'em in a ferment. Contemplation requires a Governable Body, a sedate and steady Mind, and the Body and the Mind do so reciprocally influence each other, that we can scarce keep the one in tune if the other be out of it. We can neither Observe the Errors of our Intellect, nor the Irregularity of our Morals whilst we are darkned by Fumes, agitated with unruly Passions, or carried away with eager Desires after Sensible things and vanities. We must therefore withdraw our Minds from the World, from adhering to the Senses, from the Love of Material Beings, of Pomps and Gaieties; for 'tis these that usually Steal away the Heart, that seduce the Mind to such unaccountable Wandrings, and so fill up its Capacity that they leave no room for Truth, so distract its Attention that it cannot enquire after her. For tho' the Body does partly occasion this fault, yet the Will no doubt may in good measure Remedy it by using its Authority to fix the Understanding on such Objects as it wou'd have Contemplated; it has a Rein which will certainly curb this wandring, if it can but be persuaded to make use of it. Indeed Attention and deep Meditation is not so agreeable to our Animal Nature, does not flatter our Pride so well as this agreeable Reverie, which gives us a pretence to Knowledge without taking much Pains to acquire it, and does not choak us with the humbling thoughts of our own Ignorance, with which we must make such ado e're it can be enlightened. Yet without Attention and strict Examination we are liable to false Judgments on every occasion, to Vanity and Arrogance, to Impertinent Prating of things we don't understand, are kept from making a Progress, because we fancy our selves to be at the top already, and can never attain to true Wisdom. If then we wou'd hereafter think to purpose, we must suffer our selves to be convinc'd how oft we have already thought to none, suspect our Quickness, and not give our desultory Imagination leave to ramble.

And in order to the restraining it we may consider, what a loss of Time and Study such irregular and useless Thoughts occasion, what a Reproach they are to our Reason, how they cheat us with a *shew* of Knowledge, which so long as we are under the power of this giddy Temper will inevitably escape us. And if to this we add a serious perusal of such Books as are not loosly writ, but require an Attent and Awakened Mind to apprehend, and to take in the whole force of 'em, obliging our selves to Understand them throughly, so as to be able to give a just account of them to our Selves, or rather to some other Person intelligent enough to take it and to correct our mistakes, it is to be hop'd we shall obtain a due poise of Mind, and be able to direct our Thoughts to the thorow discussion of such Subjects as we wou'd Examine. Such Books I mean as are fuller of Matter than Words, which diffuse a light through every part of their Subject, do not Skim, but Penetrate it to the bottom, yet so as to leave somewhat to be wrought out by the Reader's own Meditation; such as are writ with Order and Connexion, the Strength of whose Arguments can't be sufficiently felt unless we remember and compare the whole System. 'Tis impossible to prescribe absolutely, and every one may easily find what Authors are most apt to stay their Attention, and shou'd apply to them. But whenever they Meditate, be it on what Object it may, let 'em fix their Minds stedily on it, not removing till it be throughly Examin'd, at least not until they have seen all that's necessary to their present purpose.

Doing so we shall prevent Rashness and Precipitation in our Judgments, which is occasion'd by that Volatileness we have been speaking of, together with an over-weaning opinion of our Selves. All the irregularities of our Will proceed from those false Judgments we make, thro want of Consideration, or a partial Examination when we do consider. For did we Consider with any manner of Attention, we cou'd not be so absurd as to call Evil, Good, and Chuse it as such, or prefer a less Good before a greater, a poor Momentary Trifle before the Purity and Perfection of our Mind, before an Eternal and Immutable Crown of Glory! But we seek no farther than the first Appearances of

Truth and Good, here we Stop, allowing neither Time nor Thought to search to the bottom, and to pull off those Disguises which impose on us. This Precipitation is that which gives birth to all our Errors, which are nothing else but a hasty and injudicious Sentence, a mistaking one thing for another, supposing an Agreement or Disparity amongst Ideas and their Relations where in reality there is none, occasion'd by an imperfect and cursory view of 'em. And tho' there are other things which may be said to lead us into Error, yet they do it only as they seduce us into Rash and Precipitate Judgments. We love Grandeur and every thing that feeds our good Opinion of our Selves, and therefore wou'd Judge off hand, supposing it a disparagement to our Understandings to be long in Examining, so that we greedily embrace whatever seems to carry Evidence enough for a speedy Determination, how slight and superficial soever it be. Whereas did we calmly and deliberately Examine our Evidence, and how far those Motives we are acted by ought to Influence, we shou'd not be liable to this Seduction. For hereby the Impetuosity of a warm Imagination wou'd be cool'd, and the extravagancies of a Disorderly one Regulated; we shou'd not be Deceiv'd by the Report of our Senses; the Prejudices of Education; our own Private Interest, and readiness to receive the Opinions whether True or False of those we Love, and wou'd appear to Love because we think they will serve us in that Interest; our inordinate thirst after a great Reputation, or the Power and Riches, the Grandeurs and Pleasures of this World, these wou'd no longer dissipate our Thoughts and distract our Attention, for then we shou'd be sensible how little Concern is due to them. We shou'd neither mistake in the End and Object by not employing our Understandings at All about such things as they were chiefly made for, or not Enough, or by busying them with such as are out of their reach, or beneath their Application; nor shou'd we be out in the Method of our Meditation, by going a wrong or a round about way. For the GOD of Truth is ready to lead us into all Truth, if we Honestly and Attentively apply our selves to him.

In sum, whatever false Principle we embrace, whatever wrong Conclusion we draw from true ones, is a disparagement to our Thinking Power, a Weakness of Judgment proceeding from a Confuse and Imperfect view of things, as that does from want of attention, and a hasty and partial Examination. It were endless to reckon up all the false Maxims and Reasonings we fall into, nor is it possible to give a List of them, for there are innumerable Errors opposite to one single Truth. The General Causes have been already mention'd, the Particulars are as many as those several Compositions which arise from the various mixtures of the Passions, Interests, Education, Conversation and Reading, &c. of particular Persons. And the best way that I can think of to Improve the Understanding, and to guard it against all Errors proceed they from what Cause they may, is to regulate the Will, whose Office it is to determine the Understanding to such and such Ideas, and to stay it in the Consideration of them so long as is necessary to the Discovery of Truth; for if the Will be right the Understanding can't be guilty of any Culpable Error. Not to Judge of any thing which we don't Apprehend, to suspend our Assent till we see just Cause to give it, and to determine nothing till the Strength and Clearness of the Evidence oblige us to it. To withdraw our selves as much as may be from Corporeal things, that pure Reason may be heard the better; to make that use of our Senses for which they are design'd and fitted, the preservation of the Body, but not to depend on their Testimony in our Enquiries after Truth. Particularly to divest our selves of mistaken Self-love, little Ends and mean Designs, and to keep our Inclinations and Passions under Government. Not to engage our selves so far in any Party or Opinion as to make it in a manner necessary that that shou'd be Right, lest from wishing it were, we come at last to persuade our selves it is so. But to be passionately in Love with Truth, as being throughly sensible of her Excellency and Beauty. To embrace her how opposite soever she may sometimes be to our Humours and Designs, to bring these over to her, and never attempt to make her truckle to them. To be so far from disliking a Truth because it touches us home, and lances our tenderest and dearest Corruption, as on the contrary to prize it the more, by how much the more plainly it shews us our Errors and Miscarriages. For indeed it concerns us most to know such Truths as these, it is not material to us what other Peoples Opinions are, any farther than as the Knowledge of their Sentiments may correct Our Mistakes. And the higher our Station is in the World, so much the greater need have we to be curious in this particular.

The mean and inconsiderable often stumble on Truth when

they seek not after her, but she is commonly kept out of the way, and industriously conceal'd from the Great and mighty; either out of Design or Envy, for whoever wou'd make a Property of another must by all means conceal the Truth from him; and they who Envy their Neighbours Preeminence in other things, are willing themselves to excel in exactness of Judgment, which they think and very truly, to be the greatest Excellency. And to help forward this deception, the Great instead of being Industrious in finding out the Truth, are generally very impatient when they meet with her. She does not treat them so tenderly and fawningly, with so much Ceremony and Complaisance as their Flatterers do. There's in her that which us'd to be the Character of our Nation, and honest Plainness and Sincerity, Openness and blunt Familiarity: She cannot mould her self into all Shapes to be rendred agreeable, but standing on her Native Worth is regardless of Out-side and Varnish. But to return from this Digression.

Above all things we must be throughly convinc'd of our entire Dependance on GOD, for what we *Know* as well as for what we Are, and be warmly affected with the Sense of it, which will both Excite us to Practise, and Enable us to Perform the rest. Tho' we are Naturally Dark and Ignorant, yet in *his Light, we may* hope to *see Light,* if with the Son of *Syrac* we Petition for *Wisdom that sits by his Throne* to *labour with us,* and Sigh with *David* after his *Light and Truth.* For then he who is *The Light that Lightneth every one who comes into the World,* the Immutable Truth, and Uncreated Wisdom of His Father, will *Teach us in the way of Wisdom and lead us in right Paths,* he will instruct us infinitely better by the right use of our own Faculties than the brightest Human Reason can. For in him are all the Treasures of Wisdom and Knowledge which he Liberally dispences to all who Humbly, Honestly and Heartily ask 'em of him. To close this Head: Whatever the Notion That we see all things in GOD, may be as to the Truth of it, 'tis certainly very commendable for its Piety, in that it most effectually humbles the most dangerous sort of Pride, the being Proud of our Knowledge, and yet does not slacken our Endeavours after Knowledge but rather Excites them.

IV. As to the *Method* of Thinking, if it be proper for me to say any thing of that, after those better Pens which have treated of it already, it falls in with the Subject I'me now come to, which is, that *Natural Logic* I wou'd propose. I call it natural because I shall not send you further than your Own Minds to learn it, you may if you please take in the assistance of some well chosen Book, but a good Natural Reason after all, is the best Director, without this you will scarce Argue well, tho you had the Choicest Books and Tutors to Instruct you, but with it you may, tho' you happen to be destitute of the other. For as a very Judicious Writer *Art* on this Subject (to whose Ingenious Remarks and Rules I am *of* much obliged) well observes, "These Operations (of the Mind) *Think-* proceed meerly from Nature, and that sometimes more perfectly *ing* from those who are altogether ignorant of Logic, than from others who have learn'd it."

That which we propose in all our Meditations and Reasonings is, either to deduce some Truth we are in search of, from such Principles as we're already acquainted with; or else, to dispose our Thoughts and Reasonings in such a manner, as to be able to Convince others of those Truths which we our selves are Convinc'd of. Other Designs indeed Men may have, such as the Maintenance of their Own Opinions, Actions and Parties without regard to the Truth and Justice of 'em, or the Seduction of their unwary Neighbours, but these are Mean and Base ones, beneath a Man, much more a Christian, who is or Ought to be endow'd with greater Integrity and Ingenuity.

Now Reasoning being nothing else but a Comparison of Ideas, and a deducing of Conclusions from Clear and Evident Principles, it is in the first place requisite that our Ideas be Clear and Just, and our Principles True, else all our Discourse will be Nonsense and Absurdity, Falsehood and Error. And that our Idea may be Right, we have no more to do but to look attentively into our Minds, having as we said above, laid aside all Prejudices and whatever may give a false tincture to our Light, there we shall find a Clear and Lively Representation of what we seek for, unsophisticated with the Dross of false Definitions and unintelligible Expressions. But we must not imagine that a transient view will serve the turn, or that our Eye will be Enlightened if it be not fix'd. For tho' Truth be exceeding bright, yet since our Prejudices and Passions have darkned our Eye-sight, it requires no little Pains and Application of Mind to find her out, the neglect of which Application is the Reason that we have so little Truth, and that the little we have is almost lost in that Rubbish of Error which is mingled with it. And since Truth is so near at hand, since we are not oblig'd to tumble over many Authors, to hunt after every celebrated Genius, but may have it for enquiring after in our own Breasts, are we not inexcusable if we don't obtain it? Are we not unworthy of Compassion if we suffer our Understandings to be overrun with Error? Indeed it seems to me most Reasonable and most agreeable to the Wisdom and Equity of the Divine Operations, that every one shou'd have a Teacher in their own Bosoms, who will if they seriously apply themselves to him, immediately Enlighten them so far as that is necessary, and direct them to such Means as are sufficient for their Instruction both in Humane and Divine Truths; for as to the latter, Reason if it be Right and Solid, will not pretend to be our sole Instructor, but will send us to Divine Revelation when it may be had.

GOD does nothing in vain, he gives no Power or Faculty which he has not allotted to some proportionate use, if therefore he has given to Mankind a Rational Mind, every individual Understanding ought to be employ'd in somewhat worthy of it. The Meanest Person shou'd Think as *Justly*, tho' not as *Capaciously*, as the greatest Philosopher. And if the Understanding be made for the Contemplation of Truth, and I know not what else it can be made for, either there are many Understandings who are never able to attain what they were design'd and fitted for, which is contrary to the Supposition that GOD made nothing in Vain, or else the very meanest must be put in a way of attaining it: Now how can this be if all that which goes to the composition of a Knowing Man in th' account of the World, be necessary to make one so? All have not leisure to Learn Languages and pore on Books, nor Opportunity to Converse with the Learned; but all may *Think*, may use their own Faculties rightly, and consult the Master who is within them.

By Ideas we sometimes understand in general all that which is the immediate Object of the Mind, whatever it Perceives; and in this large Sense it may take in all Thought, all that we are any ways capable of Discerning: So when we say we have no Idea of a thing, 'tis as much as to say we know nothing of the matter. Again, it is more strictly taken for that which represents to the Mind some Object distinct from it, whether Clearly or Confusedly; when this is its import, our Knowledge is said to be as Clear as our Ideas are. For that Idea which represents a thing so

Clearly, that by an Attent and Simple View we may discern its Properties and Modifications, at least so far as they can be Known, is never false; all our Certainty and Evidence depends on it, if we Know not Truly what is thus represented to our Minds we know nothing. Thus the Idea of Equality between 2 and 2 is so evident that it is impossible to doubt of it, no Arguments could convince us of the Contrary, nor be able to persuade us that the same may be found between 2 and 3.

And as such an Idea as this is never False, so neither can any Idea be said to be so, if by False we mean that which has no Existence; our Idea certainly Exists, tho' there be not any thing in Nature Correspondent to it. For tho' there be no such thing as a Golden Mountain, yet when I think of one, 'tis certain I have an Idea of it.

But our Ideas are then said to be False, or rather Wrong, when they have no Conformity to the Real Nature of the Thing whose Name they bear. So that properly Speaking it is not the Idea but the Judgment that is False; we err in supposing that our Idea is answerable to something without us when it is not. In simple Perceptions we are not often deceiv'd, but we frequently mistake in Compounding them, by Uniting several things which have no Agreement, and Separating others which are Essentially United. Indeed it may happen that our Perceptions are faulty sometimes, thro the Indisposition of the Organs or Faculties, thus a Man who has the *Jaundice* sees every thing ting'd with Yellow, yet even here the Error is not in the Simple Idea but in the Compos'd one, for we do not mistake when we say the Object appears Yellow to our Sight, tho' we do, when we affirm that it does, or ought to do so to others. So again, when the Mind does not sufficiently Attend to her Ideas nor Examine them on all sides, 'tis very likely she will Think amiss, but this also is a false Judgment, that which is amiss in the Perception being rather the Inadequateness than the Falshood. Thus in many Cases we enquire no farther than whether an Action be not Directly Forbidden, and if we do not find it Absolutely Unlawful, we think that sufficient to Authorize the Practise of it, not considering it as we ought to do, Cloathed with the Circumstances of Scandal, Temptation, &c. which place it in the same Classes with things unlawful, at least make it so to us.

Rational Creatures shou'd endeavour to have right Ideas of

every thing that comes under their Cognizance, but yet our Ideas of Morality, our thoughts about Religion are those which we shou'd with greatest speed and diligence rectifie, because they are of most importance, the Life to come, as well as all the Occurences of This, depending on them. We shou'd search for Truth in our most abstracted Speculations, but it concerns us nearly to follow her close in what relates to the Conduct of our Lives. For the main thing we are to drive at in all our Studies, and that which is the greatest Improvement of our Understandings is the Art of Prudence, the being all of a Piece, managing all our Words and Actions as it becomes Wise Persons and Good Christians.

Yet in this we are commonly most faulty; for besides the deceits of our Passions, our Ideas of Particular Vertues and Vices, Goods and Evils, being an assemblage of divers simple Perceptions, and including several Judgments are therefore liable to mistake, and much more so considering how we commonly come by them. We hear the Word that Stands for such a Thing, suppose Honor, and then instead of enquiring what it is at the Fountain head the Oracles of GOD, and our own, or the Impartial Reason of the Wisest and the Best, Custom and the Observations we make on the Practice of such as Pretend to it forms our Idea, which is seldom a Right one, the Opinions and Practices of the World being very fallacious, and many times quite opposite to the Dictates of Reason wou'd we but give ear to them. For what a strange distorted Idea of Honor must they needs have, who can think it Honourable to break a Vow that ought to be Kept, and Dishonourable to get loose from an Engagement that ought to be Broken? Who cannot endure to be tax'd with a Lye, and yet never think fit to keep their Word? What do they think of Greatness who support their Pomp at the Expence of the Groans and Tears of many Injur'd Families? What is their Idea of Heaven, who profess to Believe such a thing, and yet never endeavour to Qualifie themselves for the Enjoyment of it? Have they any Idea at all of these things when they speak of 'em? Or, if they have, is it not a very false one?

Now that we may avoid mistake the better, and because we usually join Words to our Ideas even when we only Meditate, we shou'd free them from all Equivocation, not make use of any Word, which has not a Distinct Idea annex'd to it, and where Custom has join'd many Ideas to one Word, carefully separate and distinguish them. For if our Words are Equivocal, how can we by Pronouncing such and such, excite the same Idea in another that is in our own Mind, which is the End of Speech, and consequently how can we be Understood? And if sometimes we annex one Idea to a Word, and sometimes another, we may for ever wrangle with those who perhaps wou'd be found to agree with us if we Understood each other, but can neither Convince them, nor clear up the Matter to our own Mind. For Instance: Shou'd I dispute Whether Evil were to be Chosen? Without defining what I mean by Evil, which is a Word customarily apply'd to things of different Natures, and shou'd conclude in the Affirmative, meaning at the same time the Evil of Pain, or any Corporal Loss or Punishment, I were not mistaken, tho' another Person who annexes no other Idea but that of Sin to the word Evil, might Justly contradict me and say that I was. Or if in the Process of my Discourse, I shou'd without giving notice of it, substitute the Idea of Sin instead of that of Pain, when I mention Evil, I shou'd argue falsely. For it is a Maxim that we may Chuse a less Evil to avoid a greater, if both of them be Corporal Evils, or if one of them be so, and we chuse it to avoid Sin, between which and the Evil of Pain there is no Comparison: But if the two Evils propos'd to our Choice be both of them Sinful, that Principle will not hold, we must Chuse neither, whatever comes on't, Sin being Eligible no manner of way.

Thus many times our ideas are thought to be false when the fault is really in our Language, we make use of Words without joyning any, or only loose and indeterminate Ideas to them, Prating like Parrots who can Modify Sounds, and Pronounce Syllables, and sometimes martial them as a Man wou'd, tho' without the use of Reason or understanding any thing by them. So that after a long Discourse and many fine Words, our Hearer may justly ask us what we have been saying? And what it is we wou'd be at? And so a great part, of the Good Breeding of the World, many Elegant Complements pass for nothing, they have no meaning, or if they have, 'tis quite contrary to what the Words in other Cases signifie.

From the Comparison of two or more Ideas clearly Conceived arises a Judgment, which we may lay down for a Principle, and as we have occasion Argue from. Always observing that those Judgments which we take for Axioms or Principles, be such as carry the highest Evidence and Conviction, such as every one who will but in the least Attend may Clearly see, and be fully convinced of, and which need not another Idea for their Demonstration. Thus from the Agreement which we plainly perceive between the Ideas of GOD and of Goodness singly consider'd, we discern that they may be joyn'd together so as to form this Proposition, *That GOD is Good:* And from the evident disparity that is between GOD and Injustice, we learn to affirm this other, *That he is not Unjust.* And so long as we Judge of Nothing but what we see Clearly, we can't be mistaken in our Judgments, we may indeed in those Reasonings and Deductions we draw from them, if we are Ignorant of the Laws of Argumentation, or Negligent in the Observation of them.

The First and Principal thing therefore to be observed in all the Operations of the Mind is, That we determine nothing about those things of which we have not a Clear Idea, and as Distinct as the Nature of the Subject will permit, for we cannot properly be said to Know any thing which does not Clearly and Evidently appear to us. Whatever we see Distinctly we likewise see Clearly, Distinction always including Clearness, tho this does not necessarily include that, there being many Objects Clear to the view of the Mind, which yet can't be said to be Distinct.

Les Princip. de la Philos. de M. Des Cartes. Part I, para. 45 That (to use the Words of a Celebrated Author) may be said to be "Clear which is Present and Manifest to an attentive Mind; so as we say we see Objects Clearly, when being present to our Eyes they sufficiently Act on 'em, and our Eyes are dispos'd to regard 'em. And that Distinct, which is so Clear, Particular, and Different from all other things, that it contains not any thing in it self which appears not manifestly to him who considers it as ought." Thus we may have a Clear, but not a Distinct and Perfect Idea of GOD and of our own Souls; their Existence and some of their Properties and Attributes may be Certainly and Indubitably Known, but we can't Know the Nature of our Souls Distinctly, for Reasons too long to be mentioned here, and less that of GOD, because he is Infinite. Now where our Knowlege is Distinct, we may boldly deny of a subject, all that which after a careful Examination we find not in it: But where our Knowledge is only Clear, and not Distinct, tho' we may safely Affirm what we see, yet we can't without a hardy Presumption Deny of it what we see not. And were it not very common to find People both Talking and Writing of things of which they have no Notion, no Clear Idea; nay and determining Dogmatically concerning the intire Nature of those of which they cannot possibly have an Adequate and Distinct one, it might seem Impertinent to desire them to speak no farther than they Apprehend. They will tell you Peremptorily of Contradictions and Absurdities in such matters as they themselves must allow they cannot Comprehend, tho others as Sharp sighted as themselves can see no such thing as they complain of.

As Judgments are form'd by the Comparing of Ideas, so Reasoning or Discourse arises from the Comparison or Combination of several Judgments. Nature teaches us when we can't find out what Relation one Idea bears to another by a Simple view or bare Comparison, to seek for a Common Measure or third Idea, which Relating to the other two, we may by Comparing it with each of 'em, discern wherein they agree or differ. Our Invention discovers it self in proposing readily apt Ideas for this Middle Term, our Judgment in making Choice of such as are Clearest and most to our purpose, and the excellency of our Reasoning consists in our Skill and Dexterity in Applying them.

Invention indeed is the hardest part, when Proofs are found it is not very difficult to manage them. And to know precisely wherein their Nature consists, may help us somewhat in our enquiries after 'em. An Intermediate Idea then which can make out an Agreement between other Ideas, must be Equivalent to, and yet Distinct from those we compare by it. Where Ideas agree it will not be hard to find such an Equivalent, and if after diligent search we cannot meet with any, 'tis a pretty sure Sign that they do not agree. It is not necessary indeed that our Middle Idea be Equivalent in all respects, 'tis enough if it be in such as make the Comparison: And when it is so to one of the Compar'd Ideas but not to the other, that's a Proof that they do not agree amongst themselves.

All the Commerce and Intercourse of the World is manag'd by Equivalents, Conversation as well as Traffick. Why do we Trust our Friends but because their Truth and Honesty appears to us Equivalent to the Confidence we repose in 'em? Why do we perform Good Offices to others, but because there's a proportion between them and the Merit of the Person, or our own Circumstances? And as the way to know the Worth of things is to

Compare them one with another, so in like manner we come to the Knowlege of the Truth of 'em by an Equal Ballancing. But you will say, Tho I may learn the value of a *Spanish* Coin by Weighing, or Comparing it with some other Money whose Standard I know, and so discern what proportion it bears to those Goods I wou'd exchange; yet what Scales shall I find to weigh Ideas? What Hand so even as to poize them Justly? Or if that might be done, yet where shall I meet with an Equivalent Idea when I have occasion to use one?

In answer to this Demand I consider, that as Light is always visible to us if we have an Organ to receive it, if we turn our Eyes towards it, and that nothing interpose between it and us; so is Truth, we are surrounded with it, and GOD has given us Faculties to receive it. If it be ask'd, Why then do we so seldom find it? The Reason is, because instead of making right use of our Faculties we employ them in keeping it out; we either shut our Eyes, or if we vouchsafe to open them, we are sure to view it thro such unsuitable Mediums as fail not to misrepresent it to us. As for those few Noble Spirits, who open the Windows of their Souls to let in Truth, and take the Films of Interest, Passion and Prejudice from before their Eyes, they will certainly be Enlighten'd, and cannot miss of obtaining as much Truth as they are capable of Receiving. For, to go on with the Comparison, as we can See no farther than our own Horizon, tho the Light shine never so bright around us; and as we cannot discern every Object even within that Compass Clearly, nor Any Distinctly but what we particularly apply our selves to; So neither are our Capacities large enough to take in *All* Truth, as has been often said, nor are we capable of attaining *Any* without Attention and diligent Examination. But if we carefully Consider those Ideas we already have and Attend to those Truths we are acquainted with, we cannot want Mediums to discover more, if our Enquiries be after that which is within our Reach. He who is the Fountain of Truth is also a GOD of Order, and has so regularly connex'd one Truth with another, that the discovery of one is a step towards a further Progress; so that if we diligently Examine those Truths which, we Know, they will clear the way to what we search after: For it seldom happens but that the Question it self directs us to some Idea that will serve for the Explanation or Proof of it.

There is no Object, no Accident of Life but affords us matter of Instruction. GOD has so dispos'd all the Works of his Hands, all the Actings of his Providence, that every one of 'em ministers to our Improvement, if we will but Observe and Apply them. Indeed this Living *Ex Tempore* which most of us are guilty of, our making no Reflections, our Gay and Volatile Humour which transports us in an Instant from one thing to another, e're we have with the Industrious Bee suck'd those Sweets it wou'd afford us, frequently renders his gracious Bounty ineffectual. For as the Diligent hand maketh Rich, whil'st the Slothful and Prodigal come to nothing, so the Use of our Powers improves and Encreases them, and the most Observing and Considerate is the Wisest Person: For she lays up in her Mind as in a Store-house, ready to produce on all Occasions, a Clear and Simple Idea of every Object that has at any time presented it self. And perhaps the difference between One Womans Reason and anothers may consist only in this, that the one has amass'd a greater number of such Ideas than the other, and dispos'd them more Orderly in her Understanding, so that they are at hand, ready to be apply'd to those Complex Ideas whose Agreement or Disagreement cannot be found out but by the means of some of 'em.

But because Examples are more familiar than Precepts, as condescending to shew us the very manner of Practising them, I shall endeavour to make the matter in Hand as plain as I can by subjoining Instances to the following Rules, which Rules as I have not taken wholly on Trust from others, so neither do I pretend to be the Inventer of 'em.

We have heard already that a Medium is necessary when we can't discern the Relation that is between two or more Ideas by Intuition or a simple View. Could this alone procure us what we seek after, the addition of other Ideas wou'd be needless, since to make a shew of Wit by tedious Arguings and unnecessary Flourishes, does only Perplex and Incumber the Matter, Intuition being the Simplest, and on that account the best way of Knowing.

Rule I. And therefore we shou'd in the first place, *Acquaint our selves throughly with the State of the Question, have a Distinct Notion of our Subject whatever it be, and of the Terms we make use of, knowing precisely what it is we drive at*: that so we may in the second

Rule II. *Cut-off all needless Ideas and whatever has not a Connexion to the matter under Consideration,* which serve only to fill up the Capacity of the Mind, and to Divide and Distract the Attention. From the neglect of this comes those causless Digressions, tedious Parentheses and Impertinent Remarques which we meet with in some Authors. For, as when our Sight is diffus'd and extended to many Objects at once we see none of them Distinctly; so when the Mind grasps at every Idea that presents it self, or rambles after such as relate not to its Present Business, it loses its hold and retains a very feeble Apprehension of that which it shou'd Attend. Some have added another Rule (*viz.*) *That we Reason only on those things of which we have Clear Ideas;* but I take it to be a Consequence of the first, and therefore do not make it a distinct one: For we can by no means Understand our Subject, or be well acquainted with the State of the Question, unless we have a Clear Idea of all its Terms.

Rule III. Our Business being stated, the next Rule is *To conduct our Thoughts by Order, beginning with the most Simple and Easie Objects, and ascending as by Degrees to the Knowledge of the more Compos'd.* I need not tell you, that Order makes every thing, Easie, Strong and Beautiful, and that the Superstructure is neither like to Last or Please unless the Foundation be duly laid, for this is obvious to the most Superficial Reader. Nor are they likely to solve the Difficult, who have neglected or slightly pass'd over the Easie Questions. Our Knowledg is gradual, and by passing Regularly thro Plain things, we arrive in due time at the more Abstruse.

Rule IV. In this Method we are to practise the Fourth Rule which is, *Not to leave any part of our Subject unexamin'd,* it being as necessary to Consider All that can let in Light, as to shut out what's Foreign to it. We may stop short of Truth as well as over-run it; and tho we look never so attentively on our proper Object, if we view but half of it, we may be as much mistaken, as if we extended our Sight beyond it. Some Objects agree very well when observ'd on one side, which upon turning the other shew a great disparity. Thus the Right Angle of a Triangle may be like to one part of a Square, but compare the Whole, and you'l find 'em very different Figures. And a Moral Action may in some Circumstance be not only Fit but Necessary, which in others, where Time, Place, and the like have made an alteration, wou'd be most Improper; so that if we venture to Act on the former Judgment, we may easily do amiss, if we wou'd Act as we ought, we must view its New Face, and see with what Aspect that looks on us.

To this Rule belongs that of *Dividing the Subject of our Meditations into as many Parts, as we can, and as shall be requisite to Understand it perfectly.* This is indeed most necessary in difficult Questions, which will scarce be unravell'd but in this manner by Pieces: Ever taking care to make Exact Reviews, and to Sum up our Evidence justly e're we pass Sentence and fix our Judgment.

Rule V. To which purpose we must *Always keep our Subject Directly in our Eye, and Closely pursue it thro all our Progress;* there being no better Sign of a good Understanding than Thinking Closely and Pertinently, and Reasoning dependently, so as to make the former part of our Discourse a support to the Latter, and *This* an Illustration of *That,* carrying Light and Evidence in ev'ry step we take. The neglect of this Rule is the Cause why our Discoveries of Truth are seldom Exact, that so much is often said to so little purpose; and many Intelligent and Industrious Readers when they have Read over a book are very little wiser than when they began it. And that the two last Rules may be the better observ'd, 'twill be fit very often to look over our Process so far as we have gone, that so by rendring our Subject Familiar, we may the sooner arrive to an Exact Knowlege of it.

Rule VI. All which being done we are in a fair way towards keeping the last Rule, which is, *To judge no further than we Perceive, and not to take any thing for Truth which we do not evidently Know to be so.* Indeed in some Cases we are forc'd to content our selves with Probability, but 'twere well if we did so only where 'tis plainly Necessary. That is, when the Subject of our Meditation is such as we cannot possibly have a Certain Knowlege of, because we are not furnish'd with Proofs which have a Constant and Immutable Connexion with the Ideas we apply them to, or because we can't perceive it, which is our Case in such Exigencies as oblige us to Act presently, on a cursory view of the Arguments propos'd to us, when we want time to trace them to the bottom, and to make use of such means as wou'd discover Truth.

I cannot think we are often driven to such straits in any considerable Affair, tho I believe that very many Subjects may be propos'd to us, concerning which we cannot readily pass our Judgment, either because we never consider'd them before, or because we are wanting in some Means that lead to the Knowlege of 'em. In which Case Reason wills that we suspend our Judgment till we can be better Inform'd; nor wou'd it have us remit our Search after Certainty, even in those very Cases in which we may sometimes be forc'd to Act only on Probable Grounds. For Reason can't rest satisfy'd with Probabilities where Evidence is possible, our Passions and Interest may, but *That* does not incline us to leave off Enquiring lest we happen to meet somewhat contrary to our Desires. No, Reason requires us to continue our Enquiries with all the Industry we can, till they've put us in Possession of Truth, and when we have found, enjoyns us to follow her, how opposite soever she may cause our Latter Actions to be to our Former. But by this we may learn (and so we may by every thing that such weak and fallible Creatures as we are perform) to think Candidly of those whose Opinions and Actions differ from our own. Because we do not know the necessity of their Affairs, nor in what ill Circumstances they are plac'd in respect of Truth.

And now to Apply what has been said; The State of the Question being Distinctly known, and certain Ideas fixt to the Terms we make use of, we shall find sometimes that the Difference which was suppos'd to be between the Things themselves, is only in words, in the divers ways we make use of to express the same Idea.

For if upon looking into our selves we discern, that these different Terms have but one and the same Idea, when we have corrected our Expressions the Controversie is at an End, and we need enquire no further. Thus, If we are ask'd *Whether GOD is Infinitely Perfect?* There needs no Intermediate Idea to compare the Idea of GOD with that of Infinite Perfection, since we may discern them on the very first view to be one and the same Idea differently express'd, which to go about to explain or prove were only to cumber with needless words, and to make what is Clear, Obscure. For we Injure a Cause instead of Defending it, by attempting an Explanation or Proof of things so Clear, that as they do not need, so perhaps they are not Capable of any.

But if it be made a Question *Whether there is a GOD, or a Being Infinitely Perfect?* We are then to Examin the Agreement between our Idea of GOD and that of Existence. Now this may be discern'd by Intuition, for upon a View of our Ideas we find that Existence is a Perfection, and the Foundation of all other Perfections, since that which has no Being cannot be suppos'd to have any Perfection. And tho the Idea of Existence is not Adequate to that of Perfection, yet the Idea of Perfection Includes that of Existence, and if *That* Idea were divided into parts, one part of it wou'd exactly agree with *This*. So that if we will allow that *Any* Being is Infinite in All Perfections, we cannot deny that that Being Exists; Existence it self being one Perfection, and such an one as all the rest are built upon.

If unreasonable Men will farther demand, *Why is it necessary that All Perfection shou'd be Centred in One Being, is't not enough that it be parcel'd out amongst many? And tho it be true that that Being who has all Perfection must needs Exist, yet where's the Necessity of an All-Perfect Being?* We must then look about for Proofs and Intermediate Ideas, and the Objection it self will furnish us with one. For those *Many* whose Particular Ideas it wou'd have joyn'd together to make a Compound one of All-Perfection, are no other than Creatures, as will appear if we consider our Idea of Particular Being and of Creature, which are so far from having any thing to distinguish 'em, that in all Points they resemble each other. Now this Idea naturally suggests to us that of Creation, or a Power of giving Being to that which before the exerting of that Power had none, which Idea if we use it as a Medium, will serve to discover to us the necessity of an All-Perfect Being.

For in the first place, what ever has any Perfection or Excellency (for that's all we mean by Perfection here) must either have it of it self, or derive it from some other Being. Now Creatures cannot have their Perfections from themselves because they have not their Being, for to suppose that they Made themselves is an Absurdity too ridiculous to be seriously refuted, 'tis to suppose them to Be and not to Be at the same time, and that when they were Nothing, they were able to do the greatest Matter. Nor can they derive either Being or Perfection from any other Creature. For tho some Particular Beings may seem to be the Cause of the Perfections of others, as the Watch-maker may be said to be the Cause of the Regular Motions of the Watch, yet trace it a little farther, and you'l find this very Cause shall need another, and so without End, till you come to the Foundation-head, to that All-Perfect Being, who is the last resort of our Thoughts, and in whom they Naturally and Necessarily rest and terminate. If to this it be Objected that we as good as affirm that this All-Perfect Being is his own Maker, by saying he is Self-Existent, and so we fall into the same Absurdity which we imputed to that Opinion which supposes that Creatures were their own Maker. The reply is easie, That we do not say he Made himself, we only affirm that his Nature is such, that tho we can't sufficiently Explain because we can't comprehend it, yet thus much we can discern, that if he did not Exist of himself no other Being could ever have Existed. So that either All must be swallow'd up in an Infinite Nothing, if Nothing can properly have that Epithet, and we must suppose, that neither we our selves, nor any of those Creatures about us ever had, or ever can have a Being, which is too ridiculous to imagine, or else we must needs have recourse to Self-Existing Being, who is the Maker and Lord of all things, And since Self Existence must of necessity be plac'd somewhere, is it not much more Natural and Reasonable to place it in Infinite Perfection, than amongst poor, frail Creatures, whose Origin we may trace, and whose End we see daily hastning?

To Sum up all: Since there are Innumerable Beings in the World, which have each of them their several Excellencies or Perfections; Since these can no more derive their Perfections than their Being from themselves or from any other Creature; Since a Self-Existing Being is the result of our Thoughts; the First and only True Cause, without whom it is impossible that any thing should ever have Existed; since Creatures with their Being receive all that depends on it from him their Maker; Since none can give what he has not, and therefore he who Communicates an innumerable variety of Perfections to his Creatures, even all that they enjoy, must needs contain in himself all those Beauties and Perfections he is pleas'd to Communicate to Inferior Beings; nothing can be more Plain and Evident than that there is a GOD, and that the Existence of an All-Perfect Being is Absolutely necessary.

Perhaps these Arguments are not in Form, I do not oblige my

Self to follow servilely the Rules of Art, nor know I what better Judges will think of 'em, but they seem to me to be Clear, Rational and Concluding, which is all I aim at. And I hope the Reader will receive from hence more light into the way of Arguing, that she cou'd have gain'd had I spent as many Pages in prescribing Rules and giving trifling Examples; which when they are known, merit only to be forgot again. But if some are better pleas'd with the usual way of Syllogism, and think an Argument cannot be rightly managed without one, for their Satisfaction we will add another Instance.

Suppose the Question were put *Whether a Rich Man is Happy?* By a Rich Man understanding one who possesses the Wealth and Good things of this World, and by Happy the Enjoyment of the Proper Good of Man. We compare the two Terms Riches and Happiness together, to discern if they be so much one and the same, that what is affirm'd of the one may be said of the other; but we find they are not. For if Riches and Happiness were terms Convertible, then all who are Happy must be Rich, and all who are Rich must be Happy, to affirm the last of which is to beg the Question, and the contrary appears by the following Argument, which makes use of *Satisfaction with ones own Condition* for the middle Idea or Common Measure.

He who is Happy is satisfied with his Condition and free from Anxious Cares and Solicitude (for these proceeding from the want of Good, he who enjoys his proper Good cannot be subject to them.) But Riches do not free us from Anxieties and Solicitude, they many times encrease them, Therefore to be Rich and to be Happy are not one and the same thing.

Again, If there are some who are Happy and yet not Rich, then Riches and Happiness are two distinct things. But a Good Poor Man is Happy (in the Enjoyment of GOD who is better to him than Thousands of Gold and Silver,) therefore Riches and Happiness are to be distinguish'd.

We may further consider, that if the Enjoyment of Riches can make a Man Happy according to our Notion of Happiness, they must be his Proper Good. Now if we compare the Idea of Riches with that which we have of Man, we shall find in the former nothing but what's Material, External and Adventitious, but our Idea of the latter represents to us somewhat that Thinks, and so is of an Immaterial and more noble Nature, a Nature altogether different from the former, and much more excellent and Superior to it; and by Consequence the less Noble cannot be the Good of the more, nor a Body or an Extended Substance, the Proper Good of the Mind, a Spiritual or Thinking Substance. So that upon the whole matter we find, that we cannot affirm a Man is Happy because he is Rich, neither can we deny it; Riches consider'd absolutely in 'emselves, neiher make a Man Happy nor hinder him from being so. They Contribute to his Happiness or they Obstruct it according to the Use he makes of 'em.

As for the Common Rules of Disputation they do more frequently Intangle than Clear a Question, nor is it worth while to know any more of them than may help to guard us from the Sophistry of those who use them, and assist us in the managing an Argument fairly, so long as it is Tenable, and till we are driven from it by the meer dint of Truth. To be able to hold an Argument Right or Wrong may pass with some perhaps for the Character of a Good Disputant, which yet I think it is not, but must by no means be allow'd to be that of a Rational Person; it belongs to such to detect as soon as may be the Fallacies of an ill one, and to establish Truth with the Clearest Evidence. For indeed Truth not Victory is what we shou'd contend for in all Disputes, it being more Glorious to be Overcome by her than to Triumph under the Banners of Error. And therefore we pervert our Reason when we make it the Instrument of an Endless Contention, by seeking after Quirks and Subtilties, abusing Equivocal Terms, and by practising the rest of those little Arts every Sophister is full of, which are of no service in the discovery of Truth, all they can do is to Ward off an Opponents blow, to make a Noise and raise a Dust, that so we may escape in the Hurry, our Foil being undiscover'd.

It were endless to reckon up all the Fallacies we put on our selves and endeavour to obtrude on others. On our selves in the first place, for however we may be pleas'd in the Contemplation of our own Craft or to use those softer Names we are apt to give it, our Acuteness and Ingenuity; who ever attempts to impose on others is first impos'd on himself, he is cheated by some of those grand Deceivers, the World, the Flesh, and the Devil, and made to believe that Vain-glory, Secular Interest, Ambition or perhaps Sensuality or Revenge, or any the like contemptible Appetites are preferable to Integrity and Truth.

Neither is it necessary to reduce the most usual Sophisms to general Heads, since that's already very well perform'd in a Book to which I'de rather refer you, than be at the trouble of Transcribing, having nothing to add but this, that if I be not mistaken, all the false Arguings enumerated there, and what others you may happen to meet with may be discover'd and avoided by the Rules already given, and do indeed proceed, so far as they relate to the Understanding, from the Non-observation of some of 'em. *Art of Thinking* Pr. 3. Ch. 19, 20.

But it is to little purpose to guard our selves against the Sophisms of the Head, if we lie open to those of the Heart. One irregular Passion will put a greater Obstacle between us and Truth, than the brightest Understanding and clearest Reasonings can easily remove. This every one of us is apt to discern in others, but we're blind to it in our selves. We can readily say that it is Pride or Obstinacy, Interest or Passion or in a word Self-love that keeps our Neighbour from Conviction, but all this while imagine our own Hearts are very clear of 'em, tho' more Impartial Judges are of another Mind.

I wish there were no Reason to think that there are some who attempt to maintain an Opinion which they know to be false, or at least which they have cause to suspect, and therefore industriously avoid what wou'd manifest their Error. 'Tis hop'd however that the greatest part of the Disputers of the World are not of this number, and that the reason why they offer their Neighbours Sophistical Arguments, is because they are not aware of it themselves; That what makes them so Positive is their firm persuasion that they are acted only by a Zeal of GOD, an honest Constancy and Stanch Integrity, tho at the very same time quite different Motives move them under these Appearances.

And indeed he must be an extraordinary good Man, a Wonder scarce produc'd in an Age, who has no Irregular Passion stirring; Who receives no Manner of Tincture from Pride and Vitious Self-Love, to which all are so prone, and which hide themselves under so many disguises; Who is got above the World it's Terrors and Allurements, has laid up his Treasure in Heaven, and is fully Contented with his Present Circumstances, let them be what they will, having made them the boundaries of his Desires; who knows how to live on a Little very happily and therefore receives no Bias from his own Conveniency, nor is weigh'd down by the dead Weight of his Appetites and Interests; which ought to be the Temper of every Person who wou'd find out Truth, and who desires to make a Right Judgment in all things.

We all pretend to this it's true, and think our selves Injur'd if it be not believ'd that we are Disinteress'd and free from Passion, that no Humour or Private End, nothing but an honest Zeal for Truth gives warmth to our Discourses; and yet it often happens that e're we Conclude them, we give just occasion to have it thought, that how large soever our Knowledge in other things may be, we are not well acquainted with our own Hearts. All which consider'd, how confidently soever we're perswaded of our own Integrity, tho we think we have penetrated to the very bottom of our Hearts, it wou'd not be amiss to suspect our selves sometimes, and to fear a Bias, even at the very instant we take care to avoid one.

For Truth being but One, and the Rational Faculties not differing in Kind but in Degree, tho there may be different Measures of Understanding, there could not be such Contradictions in Mens Opinions as we find there are, even in those who examin as well as in those who do not, were they acted only by the Love of Truth, and did not Self-Love perswade them that they shall find their own particular account by such an Opposition. I wou'd not be so understood as if I thought that in all Controversies one side must needs be Criminal, if not by Wilfully Opposing Truth, yet at least by an indulgence of such unmortifi'd Passions as estrange them from her. No, without doubt great allowances are to be made on the score of Education, Capacity, for Leisure, and Opportunity of Information we have had. But this we may venture to say, that had we but a Modest Opinion of our selves, believing it as possible for us as for those who contradict us to be mistaken, did we behave our selves answerable to such a belief; were we seriously convinc'd that nothing is so much our Interest as a readiness to admit of Truth, from what ever Hand it comes, greatest part of our Disputes wou'd have a better Issue than we generally find. At least if we cou'd not be so happy as to Convince one another, our Contests wou'd be manag'd with more Temper and Moderation, wou'd not conclude in such a breach of Charity, or at best in such a Coldness for each other, as they usually do.

If we consider wisely we shall find it to be our Present Interest as well as our Future, to do that in Reality which all of us

Pretend to, that is, to Search after and to Follow Truth. And to do it with all that Candor and Ingenuity which becomes a true Philosopher as well as a good Christian, making use of no Arguments but what we really believe, and giving them up contentedly when we meet with stronger. Our *Present Interest*, which is that which weighs most with the generality, and to which we make all other considerations give place; For what is it we Contend for? They who have such little Souls as to bait at any thing beneath the highest End, make Reputation their Aim, and with it that Authority and Wealth which usually attends it. But now Reputation cannot be acquir'd, at least not a lasting one, by Fallacious Reasonings; we may perhaps for a while get a Name by them amongst unwary Persons, but the World grows too quicksighted to be long impos'd on. If a Love of Truth do not, yet Envy and Emulation will set other heads a Work to discover our Ignorance or Fraud, they are upon the same Design, and will not suffer us to go away with the Prize undeservedly. And besides, with how ill an Aspect must he needs appear who does not Reason fairly, and by consequence, how unlike is he to gain on those who hear him? There are but three Causes to which false Arguments can be refer'd, Ignorance, Rashness, or Design, and the being suspected for any one of these hinders us very much in acquiring that Reputation, Authority or Preferment we desire. I must confess were we sure the Fallacy wou'd not be detected, and that we shou'd not lie under Suspicion of it, we might gain our point; for provided the Paint do not rub off, good Colouring may serve a present turn as well as a true Complection: But there is little reason to hope for this, because of what was just now mention'd, and for other Reasons that might be added.

Now what can be more provoking than the Idea we have of a Designing Person? of one who thinks his own Intellectuals so strong and ours so weak, that he can make us swallow any thing, and lead us where he pleases? such an one seems to have an Intention to reduce us to the vilest Slavery, the Captivation of our Understandings, which we justly reckon to be the highest Insolence. And since every one puts in for a share of Sense, and thinks he has no reason to complain of the distribution of it, whoever supposes that another has an over-weaning Opinion of his own, must needs think that he undervalues his Neighbours

Understanding, and will certainly repay him in his own Coin, and deny him those advantages he seems to arrogate.

The most we can say for our selves when the weakness of our Arguments comes to be discover'd, is that we were mistaken thro Rashness or Ignorance, which tho more pardonable than the former, are no recommending Qualities. If we argue falsely and know not that we do so, we shall be more pittied than when we do, but either way disappointed. And if we have added Rash Censures of those who are not of our Mind, Pride or Positiveness to our Errors as we cannot so handsomely Retreat so neither will so fair a Quarter be allow'd as those who Argue with Meekness, Modesty and Charity may well expect. So that when we have cast up our Account and estimated the Present Advantages that false Arguings bring us, I fear what we have got by a Pretence to Truth, won't be found to countervail the loss we shall sustain by the Discovery that it was no more. Which may induce us (if other Considerations will not) to be wary in receiving any Proposition our selves, and restrain us from being forward to impose our Sentiments on others.

After all, 'tis a melancholy reflection that a great part of Mankind stand in need of Arguments drawn from so low a Motive as Worldly Interest, to persuade them to that to which they have much greater inducements. It is strange that we shou'd need any other considerations besides the bare performance of our Duty, and those unspeakable advantages laid up for all such as do it sincerely, hereafter. When we have the Approbation of GOD and the infinite Rewards he has propos'd to those who study to recommend themselves to him, for our Encouragement, how low are we sunk if the Applause of Men and the little Trifles which they can bestow weigh any thing with us! I am therefore almost asham'd of proposing so mean a consideration, but the degeneracy of the Age requir'd it, and they who perhaps at first follow Truth as the Jews did once, for the Loaves only, may at last be attracted by its own Native Beauties.

V. As Nature teaches us Logic, so does it instruct us in Rhetoric much better than Rules of Art, which if they are good ones are nothing else but those Judicious Observations which Men of Sense have drawn from Nature, and which all who reflect on the Operations of their own Minds will find out 'emselves. The common Precepts of Rhetoric may teach us how to reduce

Ingenious ways of speaking to a certain Rule, but they do not teach us how to Invent them, this is Natures work and she does it best; there is as much difference between Natural and Artificial Eloquence as there is between Paint and True Beauty. So that as a good Author well observes, all that's useful in this Art, "is the avoiding certain evil ways of Writing and Speaking, and above all an Artificial and Rhetorical Stile compos'd of false Thoughts, Hyperboles and forc'd Figures which is the greatest fault in Rhetoric." *L'art de Pensers* p. 22.

I shall not therefore recommend under the name of Rhetoric an Art of speaking floridly on all Subjects, and of dressing up Error and Impertinence in a quaint and taking garb; any more than I did that Wrangling which goes by the name of Logic, and which teaches to dispute *for* and *against* all Propositions indefinitely whether they are True or False. It is an abuse both of Reason and Address to press 'em into the Service of a Trifle or an Untruth; and a mistake to think that any Argument can be rightly made, or any Discourse truly Eloquent that does not illustrate and inforce Truth. For the Design of Rhetoric is to remove those Prejudices that lie in the way of Truth, to Reduce the Passions to the Government of Reason; to place our Subject in a Right Light, and excite our Hearers to a due consideration of it. And I know not what exactness of Method, pure and proper Language, Figures, insinuating ways of Address and the like signify, any farther than as they contribute to the Service of Truth by rendring our Discourse Intelligible, Agreeable and Convincing. They are indeed very serviceable to it when they are duly managed, for Good Sense loses much of its efficacy by being ill express'd, and an ill stile is nothing else but the neglect of some of these, or over doing others of 'em.

Obscurity, one of the greatest faults in Writing, does commonly proceed from a want of Meditation, for when we pretend to teach others what we do not understand our selves, no wonder that we do it at a sorry rate. Tis true, Obscurity is sometimes design'd, to conceal an erroneous opinion which an Author dares not openly own, or which if it be discover'd he has a mind to evade. And sometimes even an honest and good Writer who studies to avoid may insensibly fall into it, by reason that his Ideas being become familiar to himself by frequent Meditation, a long train of 'em are readily excited in his mind, by a word or two which he's used to annex to them; but it is not so with his Readers who are perhaps strangers to his Meditations, and yet ought to have the very same Idea rais'd in theirs that was in the Authors mind, or else they cannot understand him. If therefore we desire to be intelligible to every body, our Expressions must be more plain and explicit than they needed to be if we writ only for our selves, or for those to whom frequent Discourse has made our Ideas familiar.

Not that it is necessary to express at length all the Process our Mind goes thro in resolving a Question, this wou'd spin out our Discourse to an unprofitable tediousness, the Operations of the Mind being much more speedy than those of the Tongue or Pen. But we shou'd fold up our Thoughts so closely and neatly, expressing them in such significant tho few words, as that the Readers Mind may easily open and enlarge them. And if this can be done with facility we are Perspicuous as well as Strong, if with difficulty or not at all, we're then perplext and Obscure Writers.

Scare any thing conduces more to Clearness, the great Beauty of writing, than Exactness of Method; nor perhaps to Persuasion, for by putting every thing in its proper place with due Order and Connexion, the Readers Mind is gently led where the Writer wou'd have it. Such a Stile is Easy without Softness, Copious as that signifies the omission of nothing necessary, yet not Wordy and Tedious; nor stuft with Nauseous Repetitions, which they who do nòt Think before they Write and dispose their Matter duly, can scarce avoid. The Method of Thinking has been already shewn, and the same is to be observ'd in Writing, which if it be what it ought, is nothing else but the communicating to others the result of our frequent and deep Meditations, in such a manner as we judge most effectual to convince them of those Truths which we believe. Always remembring that the most natural Order is ever best; that we must first prepare their minds by removing those Prejudices and Passions which are in our way, and then propose our Reasons with all the Clearness and Force, with all the Tenderness and Good-Nature we can.

And since the Clearness and Connexion as well as the Emphasis and Beauty of a Discourse depends in a great measure on a right use of the Particles, whoever wou'd Write well ought to inform themselves nicely in their Proprieties. An *And*, a *The*, a *But*, a *For*, &c. do very much perplex the Sense when they are misplac'd, and make the Reader take it many times quite otherwise than the Writer meant it. But this is not a place to say all that this Subject deserves; they who wou'd have much in a little may consult an Ingenious Author who has touch'd *Lock of Hum. Und. B. 3, Ch. 7.* upon't and from thence take hints to observe how these little words are applied in good Authors, and how themselves may best use them to express the several Postures of their own Minds.

In a word, I know not a more compendious way to good Speaking and Writing, than to chuse out the most excellent in either as a Model on which to form our selves. Or rather to imitate the Perfections of all, and avoid their mistakes; for few are so perfect as to be without fault, and few so bad as to have nothing good in them. A true Judgment distinguishes, and neither rejects the Good for the sake of the Bad, nor admits the Bad because of the Good that is mingled with it. No sort of Style but has its excellency and is liable to defect: If care be not taken the Sublime which subdues us with Nobleness of Thought and Grandeur of Expression, will fly out of sight and by being Empty and Bombast become contemptible. The Plain and Simple will grow Dull and Abject; the Severe dry and Rugged, the Florid vain and impertinent. The Strong instead of rousing the Mind will distract and intangle it by being Obscure; even the Easy and Perspicuous if it be too diffuse, or over delicate tires us intsead of pleasing. Good Sense is the principal thing without which all our polishing is of little Worth, and yet if Ornament be wholly neglected very few will regard us. Studied and artificial periods are not natural enough to please, they shew too much solicitude about what does not deserve it, and a loose and careless Style declares too much contempt of the Public. Neither Reason nor Wit entertain us if they are driven beyond a certain pitch, and Pleasure it self is offensive if it be not judiciously dispenc'd.

Every Author almost has some beauty or blemish remarkable in his Style from whence it takes its name; and every Reader has a peculiar tast of Books as well as meats. One wou'd have the Subject exhausted, another is not pleas'd if somewhat be not left to enlarge on in his own Meditations. This affects a Grave that a Florid Style; One is for Easiness, a second for Plainness, a third for Strength, and a fourth for Politeness. And perhaps the great secret of Writing is the mixing all these in so just a proportion that every one may tast what he likes without being disgusted by its contrary. And may find at once that by the Solidity of the Reason, the purity and propriety of Expression, and insinuating agreeableness of Address, his Understanding is Enlightned, his Affections subdued and his Will duly regulated.

This is indeed the true End of Writing, and it wou'd not be hard for every one to judge how well they had answer'd it, wou'd they but lay aside Self-Love, so much of it at least, as makes them partial to their own Productions. Did we consider our own with the same Severity, or but Indifference that we do anothers Writing, we might pass a due Censure on it, might discern what Thought was Crude or ill exprest, what Reasoning weak, what passage superfluous, where we were flat and dull, where extravagant and vain, and by Criticizing on our selves do a greater kindness to the World than we can in making our Remarques on others. Nor shou'd we be at a loss, if we were Impartial, in finding out Methods to Inform, Persuade and Please; for Human Nature is for the most part much alike in all, and that which has a good effect on us, will generally speaking have the same on others. So that to guess what success we are like to have, we need only suppose our selves in the place of those we Address to, and consider how such a Discourse wou'd operate on us, if we had their Infirmities and Thoughts about us.

And if we do so I believe we shall find, there's nothing more improper than Pride and Positiveness, nor any thing more prevalent than an innocent compliance with their weakness: Such as pretends not to dictate to their Ignorance, but only to explain and illustrate what they did or might have known before if they had consider'd it, and supposes that their Minds being employ'd about some other things was the reason why they did not discern it as well as we. For Human Nature is not willing to own its Ignorance; Truth is so very attractive, there's such a natural agreement between our Minds and it, that we care not to be thought so dull as not to be able to find out by our selves such obvious matters. We shou'd therefore be careful that nothing pass from us which upbraids our Neighbours Ignorance, but study to remove't without appearing to take notice of it, and permit 'em to fancy if they please, that we believe them as Wise and Good as we endeavour to make them. By this we gain their Affections which is the hardest part of our Work, excite their

Industry and infuse a new Life into all Generous Tempers, who conclude there's great hopes they may with a little pains attain what others think they Know already, and are asham'd to fall short of the good Opinion we have entertain'd of 'em.

And since many wou'd yeild to the Clear Light of Truth were't not for the shame of being overcome, we shou'd Convince but not Triumph, and rather Conceal our Conquest than Publish it. We doubly oblige our Neighbours when we reduce them into the Right Way, and keep it from being taken notice of that they were once in the Wrong, which is certainly a much greater satisfaction than that blaze of Glory which is quickly out, that noise of Applause which will soon be over. For the gaining of our Neighbour, at least the having honestly endeavour'd it, and the leading our own Vanity in Triumph are Real Goods and such as we shall always have the Comfort of. It is to be wish'd that such Propositions as are not attended with the Clearest Evidence were deliver'd only by way of Enquiry, since even the brightest Truth when Dogmatically dictated is apt to offend our Readers, and make them imagine their Liberty's impos'd on, so far is Positiveness from bringing any body over to our Sentiments. And besides, we're all of us liable to mistake, and few have Humility enough to confess themselves Deceiv'd in what they have confidently asserted, but think they're obliged in Honour to maintain an Opinion they've once been Zealous for, how desirous soever they may be to get rid on't, cou'd they do it handsomely. Now a Modest way of delivering our Sentiments assists us in this, and leaves us at liberty to take either side of the Question as Reason and Riper Consideration shall determine.

In short, as Thinking conformably to the Nature of Things is True Knowledge, so th' expressing our Thoughts in such a way, as most readily, and with the greatest Clearness and Life, excites in others the very same Idea that was in us, is the best Eloquence. For if our Idea be conformable to the Nature of the thing it represents, and its Relations duly stated, this is the most effectual way both to Inform and Perswade, since Truth being always amiable, cannot fail of attracting when she's plac'd in a Right Light, and those to whom we offer her, are made Able and Willing to discern her Beauties. If therefore we throughly understand our Subject and are Zealously affected with it, we shall neither want suitable words to explain, nor perswasive Methods to recommend it.

And since Piety and Vertue shou'd in spite of the mistaken Customs of the Age be the principal Theme of a Christians Conversation; that which those who bear that Sacred Name ought always to regard some way or other, even when it might be unseasonable to speak of it directly, the way to be good Orators is to be good Christians, the Practice of Religion will both instruct us in the Theory, and most powerfully inforce what we say of it. Did we truly relish the Delights of GOD's Service, we cou'd neither refrain from talking of the Pleasure, nor be so ill-natur'd as not to strive to Communicate it; and were we duly warm'd with a Zeal for his Glory and concern for our Neighbours Soul, no Figures of Rhetoric, no Art of Perswasion wou'd be wanting to us. We shou'd diligently watch for Opportunities, and carefully improve them, accommodating our Discourse to the Understanding and Genius of all we cou'd hope to do good to.

Besides, by being True Christians we have Really that Love for others which all who desire to perswade must pretend to; we've that *Probity* and *Prudence,* that *Civility* and *Modesty* which the Masters of this Art say a good Orator must be endow'd with: and have pluck'd up those Vicious Inclinations from whence the most distastful faults of Writing proceed. For why do we chuse to be Obscure but because we intend to Deceive, or wou'd be thought to see much farther than our Neighbours? One sort of Vanity prompts us to be Rugged and Severe, and so possess'd with the imagin'd Worth and Solidity of our Discourse, that we think it beneath us to Polish it: Another disposes us to Elaborate and Affected ways of Writing, to Pompous and improper Ornaments; and why are we tediously Copious but that we fancy Thought of ours is extraordinary? Contradiction is indeed for our advantage as tending to make us wiser, yet our Pride makes us impatient under it, because it seems to Lessen that Esteem and Deference we desire shou'd be paid us. Whence come those sharp Reflections, those imagin'd strains of Wit, not to be endur'd amongst Christians, and which serve not to Convince but to Provoke, whence come they but from Ill-nature or Revenge, from a Contempt of others and a desire to set forth our own Wit? Did we write less for our selves we should sooner gain our Readers, who are many times disgusted at a well writ Discourse if it carries a tang of Ostentation: And were our Temper as Christian as it ought to be, our Zeal wou'd be spent on the most Weighty things, not on little differences of Opinions.

I have made no distinction in what has been said between Speaking and Writing, because tho they are talents which do not always meet, yet there is no material difference between 'em. They Write best perhaps who do't with the gentile and easy air of Conversation; and they Talk best who mingle Solidity of Thought with th' agreableness of a ready Wit. As for *Pronunciation*, tho it takes more with some Auditors many times than Good Sense, there needs little be said of it here, since Women have no business with the Pulpit, the Bar or St. *Stephens Chapel*: And Nature does for the most part furnish 'em with such a Musical Tone, Perswasive air and Winning Address as renders their Discourse sufficiently agreeable in Private Conversation. And as to spelling which they're said to be defective in, if they don't believe as they're usually told, that its fit for 'em to be so, and that to write exactly is too Pedantic, they may soon correct that fault, by Pronouncing their words aright and Spelling 'em accordingly. I know this Rule won't always hold because of an Imperfection in our Language which has been oft complain'd of but is not yet amended; But in this case a little Observation or recourse to Books will assist us; and if at any time we happen to mistake by Spelling as we Pronounce, the fault will be very Venial, and Custom rather to blame than we.

I've said nothing of *Grammar* tho we can't Write properly if we transgress its Rules, supposing that Custom and the reading of English Books are sufficient to teach us the Grammar of our own Tongue, If we do but in any measure attend to them. And tho Women are generally accus'd of Writing false English, if I may speak my own Experience, their Mistakes are not so common as is pretended, nor are they the only Persons guilty. What they most commonly fail in is the Particles and Connexion, and that generally thro a Briskness of temper which make them forget, or Hast which will not suffer 'em to read over again what went before. And indeed, those who Speak true Grammar unless they're very Careless cannot write false, since they need only peruse what they've Writ, and consider whether they wou'd express 'emselves thus in Conversation.

But for this and for *Figures*, &c. and indeed for all that relates to this Subject, I must refer you to an Ingenious Treatise which handles it fully, and to which I'me oblig'd in great measure for what little skill I have. Observing only, that whatever it is we Treat of, our Stile shou'd be such as may keep our Readers Attent, and induce them to go to the End. Now Attention is usually fixt by Admiration, which is excited by somewhat uncommon either in the Thought or way of Expression. We fall a sleep over an Author who tells us in an ordinary manner no more than we knew before: He who wou'd Take must be Sublime in his Sense, and must cloath it after a Noble way. His Thoughts must not be superficial, such as every one may fall into at the first glance, but the very Spirits and Essence of Thinking, the sum of many hours Meditation folded up in one handsome and comprehensive Period, whose Language is Intelligible and Easy that the Readers may not lose the pleasure of the Kernel, by the pain they find in cracking the Shell. The most difficult Subject must be made easy by his way of handling it; tho his Matter may deserve a Meditation, yet his Expressions must be so Clear that he needs not be read twice to be Understood; *these* are to be Natural and Familiar, condiscending to the meanest Capacity, whilst his Thoughts are Great enough to entertain the highest. He Discourses always on a Useful Subject in a manner agreeable to it, and Pleases that he may Instruct; Nothing seems Studied in his whole Composition, yet every thing is Extraordinary, a Beautiful Harmony shining thro all its parts. No Sentence is Doubtful, no word Equivocal, his Arguments are Clear and his Images Lively; all the Ideas he excites in your Mind, as nearly resemble the thing they represent as Words can make them. Whilst th' exactness of his Method, and Force of his Reason Enlighten and Convince the Mind; the Vivacity of his Imagination and insinuating Address, gain the Affections and Conquer the Will. By the weight and closeness of the former you wou'd take him for an Angel, and the tender and affable sweetness of the last bespeaks him a Friend. He considers that as mere Florish and Rhetorick are good for nothing, so neither will bare Reason dull and heavily express'd perform any great matter, at least not on those who need it most, whose Palates being deprav'd their Medicines must be administred in a pleasing Vehicle. Since Mankind are averse to their Real Happiness, he does not only tell 'em their Duty but Interesses them in it; and thinking it not enough to run 'em down with the strength of Reason, he draws 'em over to a Voluntary Submission by th' attractives of his Eloquence. For he has a peculiar Turn and Air which animates every Period, so that the very same Truth which was dry and Unaffecting in a vulgar Authors words, Charms and Subdues you when cloath'd in his. He shews no more warmth than may convince his Readers that he's heartily persuaded of the Truths he offers them; and if it is necessary at any time to make use of Figures to give a more Lively Representation than plain Expressions cou'd, to discribe his own Passions and excite the same in others upon a just occasion, in a word to awaken a Stupid and Clear the Mind of a Prejudic'd Reader, his Figures are duly chosen and discreetly us'd. For he knows that scarce any thing speaks a greater want of Judgment than the shewing concern where there needs none, or is a worse fault in Oratory than the polishing a Wrong or a Trifling Thought, the neatness of whose dress may strike with Admiration perhaps at first sight, but upon a review it will certainly appear Contemptible. And therefore as he does not abound in Superfluous Ornaments, so neither does he reject any thing that can promote his End, which is not his own Reputation, but the Glory of his GOD and his Neighbours Edification. He considers the narrowness of the Humane Mind, and says all that is necessary but no more; Understands it so well as to know what will move and Please, and has so much command of himself as to give over when he has done enough. Yet he can exhaust the most fruitful Subject without making the Reader weary; for when he enlarges it is in Things not Words, and he mingles Variety without Confusion. All the divers excellencies of different Stiles meet in his to make up a perfect one, Strength and Ease, Solidity and Liveliness, the Sublime and Plain. He's neither so Lofty as to fly out of Sight, nor so humble as to become Creeping and Contemptible. His Strength does not make him Rugged and Perplext nor his Smoothness Weak and Nice; tho every thing is Neat, there's not a grain of Affectation; he is gratefull to the Ear, but far remov'd from jingling Cadence. Brief when there is occasion without Dryness or Obscurity, and Florid enough to entertain th' Imagination without Distracting the Mind. There's not an Antiquated or Barbarous Word to be found in him, all is Decent, Just and Natural; no peculiar or Affected Phrases, whether Courtly or

Clownish, Grave or Burlesque. For Plain and Significant Language is ever best, we have a mistaken Idea of Learning if we think to pretend to't by sending our Reader every minute to the Dictionary. Words out of the common way are only allowable when they express our Sense with greater Force than Ordinary ones cou'd, or when they are so significant as to ease us of Circumlocutions, a hard word which I cou'd not avoid without using half a dozen words.

After all, it may not be amiss to take notice that Ornaments are common to Falsehood and Truth, but Clearness and strength of Reasoning are not. They who wou'd propagate Error usually disguise it in Equivocal Terms and Obscure Phrases; they strive to engage our Passions, rather than to Convince our Reason, and carry us away in the torrent of a warm Imagination. They endeavour to refute, or if they can't do that, to Ridicule the contrary opinion, and think this Sufficient to establish their own. Being much better skill'd in pulling down former Systems than in building new ones, for it requires no great skill to Object, and there are many Truths which we're very Certain of, and yet not able to answer every Impertinent Enquiry concerning 'em. Their greatest Art is in confounding things, in giving a probable Air to what they write, in pretending to Demonstration where the nature of the Truth does not require't, and in evading it where it does. An Immoral or Heretical Discourse therefore may be *Cunningly* but not *well* writ, for we can never plead for Error and Vice with true Eloquence. We may trick 'em up in a handsom Garb, adorn 'em with quaint Expressions, and give them such a plausible turn as may enable them to do very much Mischief; but this is only a fulsom Carcass, the substance and Life are not there if Vertue and Truth are wanting.

VI. For it is to little purpose to Think well and speak well, unless we *Live well*, this is our Great Affair and truest Excellency, the other are no further to be regarded than as they may assist us in this. She who does not draw this Inference from her Studies has Thought in vain, her notions are Erroneous and Mistaken. And all her Eloquence is but an empty noise, who employs it in any other design than in gaining Proselytes to Heaven. I am therefore far from designing to put Women on a vain pursuit after unnecessary and useless Learning, nor wou'd by any means persuade them to endeavour after Knowledge cou'd I be convinc'd that it is improper for 'em. Because I know very well that tho a thing be never so excellent in it self, it has but an ill grace if it be not suitable to the Person and Condition it is apply'd to. Fine Cloaths and Equipage do not become a Beggar, and a Mechanic who must work for daily bread for his Family, wou'd be wickedly Employ'd shou'd he suffer 'em to starve whilest he's solving Mathematical Problems. If therefore Women have another Duty incumbent on 'em, and such as is inconsistent with what we here advise, we do ill to take them from it: But to affirm this is to beg the Question, and is what I will never grant till it be better prov'd than as yet it appears to be. For if the Grand Business that Women as well as Men have to do in this World be to prepare for the next, ought not all their Care and Industry to Centre here? and since the matter is of Infinite Consequence is it equitable to deny 'em the use of any help? If therefore Knowledge were but any ways Instrumental, tho at the remotest distance, to the Salvation of our Souls, it were fit to apply our selves to it; and how much more when it is so necessary, that without it we can't do any thing that's Excellent, or Practise Vertue in the most Perfect manner. For unless we Understand our Duty and the Principles of Religion, we don't perform a Rational Service, it is but by Chance that we are Good or so much as Christians. We are their Property into whose hands we fall, and are led by those who with greatest Confidence impose their Opinions on us; Are as moveable as the different Circumstances that befall us; or if we happen to be Constant in our first way, it is not Reason but Obstinacy that makes us so. A great deal of Good will be omitted, and very much Evil, or Imperfection at least, stick to us, if we are not throughly acquainted with the Law of God and the secret springs and windings of our Hearts, which is scarce to be obtain'd without much Meditation and the helps that study affords.

And as when a rash young Traveller is about to run into dangerous places beset with Theives and full of Precipices, if you have any hearty concern for his safety, you'l not think it enough barely to shew him his way, or even to tell him of the Danger, especially if the entrance seems fair and inviting and treacherous Companions are upon the watch to decoy him into it: But you'l expose it in all its frightful Circumstances, endeavour to quicken his vigilance and excite his Passions, and all little enough for his Security. So it cannot be thought sufficient that Women shou'd but just know whats Commanded and what Forbid, without being inform'd of the Reasons why, since this is not like to secure them in their Duty. For we find a Natural Liberty within us which checks at an Injunction that has nothing but Authority to back it; And tho Religion is indeed supported by the Strongest Reasons, and inforc'd by the most powerful Motives, yet if we are not acquainted with 'em, tis all one to us as if it were not. But having spoke of this in the first part we shall not farther enlarge on it here.

Perhaps it will be objected that we've said *the great Truths of Religion carry a force and Evidence suited to the very Vulgar, and that GOD has not design'd All for Philosophers.* And therefore if the way to the most necessary Knowlege be so very plain, and all Capacities are not fitted for higher attainments, what needs this ado about th' Improvements of our minds? the only thing necessary is to be good Christians, and we may be that without being Philosophers. Suppose we may; This will Justify such as want Time and Capacity, but can never excuse the Sloth and Stupidity of those who have both.

For unless we have very strange Notions of the Divine Wisdom we must needs allow that every one is placed in such a Station as they are fitted for. And if the necessity of the world requires that some Persons shou'd Labour for others, it likewise requires that others shou'd Think for them. Our Powers and Faculties were not given us for nothing, and the only advantage one Woman has above another, is the being allotted to the more noble employment. No body is plac'd without their own fault, in such unhappy Circumstances as to be incapable of Salvation, but some are plac'd in such happy ones as to be capable of attaining much greater degrees of Happiness than others if they do not neglect them: And shou'd these last do no more than the very utmost that is expected from the former, I know not how they wou'd acquit themselves, or what account they cou'd give of their great Advantages. And therefore tho no body shall be condemn'd because they *Cou'd* not, yet we have reason to fear if our Case be such as that we *Might* but *Wou'd* not receive Instruction. She then who makes this Objection must not take it amiss if we Judge of her in other Cases according to what she Pleads in this: She must never set up for a Wit, or a censurer of her Neighbours, must not pretend to be a fine Lady or any thing extraordinary: but be content to herd amongst the Drudges of the World who eat Their Bread in the Sweat of their Brows, if she says she wants Leisure; or in a less acceptable rank amongst the Fools and Ideots, or but one degree above them, if she say she wants Capacity for this Employment. It is one thing to be content with Ignorance, or rather with a less degree of Knowledge, on account of the Station that GOD has plac'd us in, and Another to Chuse and Delight in't thro a Stupid Carelesness, a fear of Trouble, or an Inordinate pursuit of the Cares and Pleasures of this Mortal Life. This last only shews our Disesteem of our Souls, our Contempt of GOD and the Talents he has given us, and exposes us to all the dreadful consequences of such a neglect; to Punishments to which not only those who misemploy their Lord's Talent, but even they who don't employ it at all, are Obnoxious.

And indeed as unnecessary as it is thought for Women to have Knowledge, she who is truly good finds very great use of it, not only in the Conduct of her own Soul but in the management of her Family, in the Conversation of her Neighbours and in all the Concerns of Life. Education of Children is a most necessary Employment, perhaps the chief of those who have any; But it is as Difficult as it is Excellent when well perform'd; and I question not but that the mistakes which are made in it, are a principal Cause of that Folly and Vice, which is so much complain'd of and so little mended. Now this, at least the foundation of it, on which in a great measure the success of all depends, shou'd be laid by the Mother, for Fathers find other Business, they will not be confin'd to such laborious work, they have not such opportunities of observing a Childs Temper, nor are the greatest part of 'em like to do much good, since Precepts contradicted by Example seldom prove effectual. Neither are Strangers so proper for it, because hardly any thing besides Paternal Affection can sufficiently quicken the Care of performing, and sweeten the labour of such a task. But Tenderness alone will never discharge it well, she who wou'd do it to purpose must throughly understand Human nature, know how to manage different Tempers Prudently, be Mistress of her own, and able to bear with all the little humours and follies of Youth, neither Severity nor Lenity are to be always us'd, it wou'd ruin some to be treated in that manner which is fit for others. As Mildness makes some ungovernable, and as there is a stupor in many from which nothing but Terrors can rouse them, so sharp Reproofs and Solemn Lectures serve to no purpose but to harden others, in faults from which they might be won by an agreeable Address and tender application. GOD himself waits to be gracious and administers his Medicines in the most proper season, and Parents shou'd imitate him in this, for the want of observing it, and of accommodating their Methods to the several Dispositions they have to deal with, is perhaps the reason that many Pious Persons lose the fruit of their Pains and Care.

Nor will Knowledge lie dead upon their hands who have no Children to Instruct; the whole World is a single Ladys Family, her opportunities of doing good are not lessen'd but encreas'd by her being unconfin'd. Particular Obligations do not contract her Mind, but her Beneficence moves in the largest Sphere. And perhaps the Glory of Reforming this Prophane and Profligate Age is reserv'd for you Ladies, and that the natural and unprejudic'd Sentiments of your Minds being handsomly express'd, may carry a more strong conviction than the Elaborate Arguments of the Learned. Such as fence themselves against the Cannon they bring down, may lie open to an Ambuscade from you. And whilst the strong arguings of the Schools like the Wind in the Fable, seems but to harden these Sturdy Sinners, your Persuasions like the Suns mild and powerful rays, may oblige them to cast off that Cloak of Maliciousness in which they are so much intangled. And surely it is worth your while to fit your selves for this: Tis a Godlike thing to relieve even the Temporal wants of our Fellow Creatures, to keep a *Body* from perishing, but it is much more Divine, to *Save a Soul from Death!* A Soul which in his estimate who best knows the value of it, is worth more than all the World. They who are thus *wise shall shine as the brightness of the Firmament, and they who turn many to Righteousness as the Stars for ever;* which is a Glory we may honestly Contend for, a Beauty we may lawfully Covet; O that we had but Ambition enough to aspire after it! O that we had but so much at least as we see daily thrown away on a poor transitory Earthly Diadem, which sets uneasy on his head who wears it, and which a longer arm may wrest from his Brows! But alas it was in our fore-fathers days that the King-

dom of Heav'n was took by violence; they thought nothing, and
we think every thing too much to Do or Suffer to obtain it!
Not but that it is still as bright and glorious, as truly attractive,
but we are dull and stupid we shut our eyes and won't behold
its Charms. Were we but duly sensible of this we shou'd think
no Posterity so desireable as the Offspring of our Minds, nor
any state so great as the carrying a large Train of Followers
with us to the Court of Heaven! So much Knowledge therefore
as is necessary to engage and keep us firm in our Christian Course,
to fit us to help others in theirs, to stir us up to pursue, and
direct us in our endeavours after one of the brightest Crowns of
Glory, does very well become us; and more than this I do not
contend for, being far from desiring that any one shou'd neglect
her Necessary Affairs to amuse her self with nice Speculations.
No; She who has a Family is discharging part of her Christian
Calling whilst She's taking care for it's Support and Government, and wou'd be very much out, if she lock'd her self in her
Study, when her Domesticks had need of her direction. But
there are few of those to whom I write, who have not a good
deal of time to spare, if you reckon whats thrown away on fan-
tastic Impertinencies, and tis this I wou'd have better employ'd:
Were not a Morning more advantageously spent at a Book than
at a Looking-Glass, and an Evening in Meditation than in Gaming?
Were not Pertinent and Ingenious Discourse more becoming in
a visit, than Idle twattle and uncharitable Remarks? than a Nauseous repetition of a set of fine words which no body believes or
cares for? And is not the fitting our selves to do Real Services
to our Neighbours, a better expression of our Civility than the
formal performance of a thousand ridiculous Ceremonies, which
every one condemns and yet none has the Courage to break
thro?

CHAP. IV.

Concerning the Regulation of the Will and the Government of the Passions.

As the Capacity which we find in our selves of Receiving and Comparing Ideas is what we call the Understanding, so the Power of Preferring any Thought or Motion, of Directing them to This or That thing rather than to another is what we mean by ·the Will: Whose Regularity consists in a constant Tendency towards such things as ought to be Prefer'd, or in a word, in Conformity to the Will of GOD. That GOD's Will is the Rule of ours is methinks so plain that it needs no proof; for why do we Prefer a thing but because we Judge it Best? and why do we Chuse it but because it Seems Good for us? Now GOD being Infinitely Wise all his Judgments must be Infallible, and being Infinitely Good he can Will nothing but what is best, nor pre-scribe any thing that is not for our Advantage. This is I dare say what every one Thinks, if they think at all about the matter, and is the Rule they wou'd Act by, did they give themselves leave upon all occasions duly to Consider and Weigh what is propos'd to them.

But as there are some Ideas which our Understandings receive so early that they seem to be born with us, which are never totally absent from our minds, and are in a manner the source of all the rest; so there are certain Motions or Inclinations in-separable from the Will, which push us on to the use of that Power, and determine it to the Choice of such things as are most agreeable to them. Nor shou'd we do amiss in following these Inclinations did they keep that Impression which the Author of Nature gave them, which is towards Good in general, or towards himself, for he only is our True Good, and these are the Wings of the Soul which shou'd carry it on vigorously towards him.

Whether there is not in us an Inclination to do what is *Fit*, that is to think and Act agreeably to a Rational Nature, without considering our own particular advantage I shall not here dispute. For whether this be so or no, tis certain that in our present Circumstances, we cannot separate *Fit* and *Good* in Reality, tho we may have distinct Ideas of them. What is really proper for Rational Creatures to do, tending necessarily to their Happiness, and nothing being able to make them truly Happy but that which is fit to be done. Besides, so pure an Inclination being wholly abstracted from Self-Love and Prejudice is not subject to any Irregularity, and so needs not be spoken of here; and perhaps so few are acquainted with it, that it will hardly be known what we mean by it.

An Inclination therefore after Happiness is that to which we shall at present reduce all the rest; which Happiness we pursue by removing as far as we can from that which is uneasie to us, and by uniting our selves as much as we are able to some Good which we suppose we want. The former of these being indeed a pursuit of Good, tho not so Directly as the latter. Good then is the Object of the Will, and hitherto one wou'd think there were no probability of our straying from the Will of GOD, and that there were so little need of advising us to Will as GOD Wills that it is impossible we shou'd Will otherwise; because whenever we oppose our Wills to his, we change in a manner the very Constitution of our Nature and fly from that Happiness which we wou'd pursue.

But the misfortune is as has been once observ'd already, that we Will e're we are capable of examining the Reasons of our Choice, or of viewing our Ideas so exactly as we must if we wou'd Judge aright. And the frequent repetition of such unreasonable Choices makes them Customary to us, and consequently gives a new and wrong bias to our Inclinations, which upon all occasions dispose the Will to the Choice of such things as we suppose, tho by mistake, to contribute to our Happiness. Add to this, that the Passions which are certain Commotions in the Bloud and Animal Spirits accompanying these Inclinations, design'd in the Order of Nature for the good of the Body, as the Inclinations were intended for the Good of the Soul, do so unite us to sensible things, and represent 'em with such advantage, that Spiritual Good which seems at a greater distance relishes very little, and abstracted Truths do not find us so Impartial as to examin them throughly, and to give them their due Weight, when they're ballanc'd against such things as may be Seen and Felt; these being commonly preferr'd, not for their intrinsic worth, but for their outward Shew and the Bulk they carry.

That we always endeavor to be Happy is sufficiently evident, and that we too frequently fly from GOD who only can make us so, Experience sadly Demonstrates. Which cou'd not be did we not grossly mistake our Happiness, as we certainly do whenever we Will any thing in opposition to the Will of GOD, whatever Appearance of Good it may happen to carry. 'Tis true the Will does always pursue Good, or somewhat represented to it as such, but it is not always, or rather very seldom, determin'd to the Choice of what is in it self the greatest Good. And though I suppose we always Chuse that which in that Juncture in which it is propos'd seems fittest for our present turn, yet it is often such as we wou'd not prefer, did we impartially examin and observe the Consequences. But we will not do that, chusing rather to Act by the Wrong Judgments we have formerly made, and to follow blindly the Propensities they have given us, than to suspend our Inclinations as we both May and Ought, and restrain them from determining our Will, till we have fairly and fully examin'd and ballanc'd, according to the best of our Knowledge, the several degrees of Good and Evil present and future that are in the Objects set before us. The neglect of which is at once both our Fault and Misery; Our Fault in that we precipitate our Choice, refusing to Consider sufficiently to rectifie our Mistakes. And our Misery because we shall certainly be Disappointed sooner or later, and be convinc'd that what was so Hastily and Unreasonably Chosen, ought not even then to have been prefer'd, how Pleasant soever it appear'd, seeing it neither Was nor Cou'd be Good for us.

It seems indeed the greatest wonder in the World how any Man in his Senses can prefer the short Pleasures of Sin, which are attended even in this Life with Pain and Shame, and a thousand Inconveniencies, to the Present Delights of Vertue, and the Prospect of a Felicity Infinite and Eternal, if he does at all compare them. An Eternity of Joys must needs be preferable to Fifty or Threescore Years of Sinful Pleasures, weigh them in what Scales you please, and supposing these much greater than ever any Sinner found 'em, especially since they are attended with

Eternal Pains, and no perverse Inclination can make us think otherwise if it will allow us to consider. But it will not allow Consideration, or if it does a little permit it, it deceives us however with fallacious Salvoes. It fixes our Thoughts on a Present Uneasiness which it says must be remov'd, and our Desires gratify'd at any rate, without suffering us to weigh the ill Consequences of doing so. And perhaps the Wrong bias which we receive from our Evil Inclinations does not consist in the persuading us that a Present Sinful Pleasure or Profit, is the Greatest Good, or that it ought to be Prefer'd before the Favour of GOD and Eternal Beatitude, which whenever we Think of we must needs acknowledge to be infinitely greater, but in keeping us from a full Conviction that th' one can't be Chosen without Renouncing th' other, and in making us unwilling to examine throughly, lest we shou'd want the pretence of Ignorance or Passion to excuse what our Consciences can't but Reproach us with as an unworthy Choice, whenever we permit our selves to Reflect.

So that the great aggravation of Sin seems to consist in this, That the commission of it is a pretending to be Wiser or Stronger than GOD, an attempt to out-wit him by Fineness, or else by plain Force to wrest his Felicity from him whether he Will or no. For seeing we always Will Happiness, and yet wou'd be Happy after another manner than GOD Wills we shall, we express a Desire, and an Endeavour so far as we're able to Oppose and Alter his Will and Order, by reconciling the gratification of a present unreasonable Appetite with the Enjoyment of Happiness, tho he has declar'd they can't be reconciled, and made it in the ordinary course of things impossible they shou'd.

The Will of GOD then is the Rule of ours, and if it be ask'd how we shall come to the Knowledg of it? the Answer is ready, that the Eternal Word and Wisdom of GOD declares his Fathers Will unto us, by *Reason* which is that Natural and Ordinary Revelation by which he speaks to every one; and by that which is call'd *Revelation* in a stricter Sense, which is nothing else but a more perfect and infallible way of Reasoning, whereby we are Clearly and Fully instructed in so much of GOD's Will as is fit for us to know. We must therefore Improve our Reason as much as our Circumstances in the World permit, and to supply its deficiency Seriously, Devoutly and Diligently study the Holy Scriptures "than which (to use the words of a most excellent

Mr.
Boyle
Style of
Scrip-
ture.
See p.
114, &c. Person) a Christian needs understand no other Book to know the duty of his Faith and Life, tho indeed to understand it well, 'tis ordinarily requisite that a pretty number of other Books be understood." In the former Chapter we have laid down a Method of using our Reason so as to discover Truth, by observing of which 'tis hop'd we may escape from considerable Errors, and consequently from great Offences. And tho I can't say we shall never be Mistaken nor Chuse amiss, yet our Infirmities will be very pitiable, such as our just and Merciful Lord God will never impute to us, tho we our selves ought to be humbled for and always endeavouring to rectifie 'em.

After all, the best way to be further Instructed in the Knowledg of our Duty is to Practise so much of it as we Know already. By keeping GOD's Commandments, we get such a sound and strong Constitution of Soul, as leads us naturally to our True Good. For as a healthy person whose Tast is not vitiated, is directed by that, without examining the Philosophy of Bodys to such things as are fit for the nourishment of his own: So a Divine Sensation gives us a lively relish of what's Good, and a perfect aversion to the contrary. It endues the Soul not only with a Sagacity of Understanding to discern readily what is best, but likewise with such a Regularity of Will, as makes it even Hate and Abhor all evil ways.

A most desirable Temper no doubt, the very top of Human Felicity, but how shall we obtain it? We find our selves under the power of quite contrary Inclinations and Relishes, and how to get rid of 'em we know not. This is indeed a very wretched condition, the only thing that deserves our Sorrow, yet the Case is not so desperate, but that by the help of an Almighty Physician we may be Cured, if in good earnest we set about it. And because the not discerning our true Happiness and the being accustom'd to pursue a false one is the cause of our Disorder, somewhat must be done by way of Meditation and somewhat by way of Exercise.

Now I know not any Subjects more proper for our Meditation on this and all occasions, than our own Nature, the Nature of Material Beings, and the Nature of GOD; because it is thro the mistake of some of these that our Inclinations take a wrong bias, and consequently that we transgress against GOD, our Neighbour and our selves. For did we consider what we Are, that Humane Nature consists in the Union of a Rational Soul with a Mortal Body, that the Body very often Clogs the Mind in its noblest Operations, especially when indulg'd. That we stand not singly on our own Bottom, but are united in some measure to all who bear a Human Form, especially to the Community amongst whom we live, and yet more particularly to those several Relations we may have in it. Did we go on to consider what are the proper Duties and Enjoyments of such a nature as ours, that is, what performances do naturally result from those Capacities we find our selves endow'd with, which may therefore be reasonably expected from us, and what sort of Pleasures we are made to relish. Again, were we so far at least Philosophers, as to be able to pass a due estimate on Material Beings, did we know 'em so well as not to prize them above their real value. Did we in the last place contemplate the Author of our Being, *from* whom we Derive and *to* whom we owe our *All;* and insted of prying saucily into his Essence, (an insufferable presumption in Creatures who are ignorant of their own) or pretending to know more of him than he has thought fit to communicate in his Word, and in that Idea of Infinite Perfection which he has giv'n ús, Frequently, Seriously and Humbly Meditate on what he has been pleas'd to unveil. Did we but employ so much of our Time and Thoughts on these things as we do on our Sins and Vanities, we shou'd not be long in discerning the good effects.

For I question not but that we shou'd be convinc'd that the Body is the Instrument of the Mind and no more, that it is of a much Inferior Nature, and therefore ought to be kept in such a Case as to be ready on all occasions to serve the Mind. That the true and proper Pleasure of Human Nature consists in the exercise of that Dominion which the Soul has over the Body, in governing every Passion and Motion according to Right Reason, by which we most truly pursue the real good of both, it being a mistake as well of our Duty as our Happiness to consider either part of us singly, so as to neglect what is due to the other. For if we disregard the Body wholly, we pretend to live like Angels whilst we are but Mortals; and if we prefer or equal it to the Mind we degenerate into Brutes. The former indeed is not frequent, it is only to be found amongst a few Scrupulous Persons, who sometimes impose such rigors on the Body, as GOD never requires at their hands, because they are inconsistent with a Human

Frame. The latter is the common and dangerous fault, for the most of us accustom our selves to tast no other Pleasures than what are convey'd to us by the Organs of Sense, we pamper our Bodies till they grow resty and ungovernable, and instead of doing Service to the Mind, get Dominion over it.

Thus we learn what is truly to Love our selves: for tho Self-Love as it is usually understood has a very ill Character and is the Root of Evil, yet rightly apply'd it is Natural and Necessary, the great inducement to all manner of Vertue. They cannot be said to Love their Body who wou'd not willingly suffer a little pain in a Finger to preserve an Arm, much more to save their Life; nor do they in reality love themselves, who wou'd not readily suffer any uneasiness in their Body, which may conduce to the good of their Mind; and who do not prefer the least probability of bettering their condition in the next Life, to all the Conveniencies of this, nay even to Life it self.

Again, when we consider that we are but several Parts of one great Whole, and are by Nature so connected to each other, that whenever one part suffers the rest must suffer with it, either by Compassion or else by being punish'd for the want of it, we shall never be so absurd as to fancy we can do our selves a Service by any thing Injurious to our Neighbours.

And finding both that we're endow'd with many excellent Faculties, which are capable of great Improvement, such as bespeak in us somewhat too Divine, to have it once imagin'd that it was made for nothing else but to move a portion of Matter 70 or 80 Years; to Act only on the Stage of an Unjust and Ill-natur'd World, where Folly and Wickedness usually go away with the Reward that is due to Wisdom and Vertue: And yet that for all these Excellencies, somewhat is still wanting to complete our Happiness, we do not find intire Felicity in our selves, but we are conscious of many wants which must be supply'd elsewhere. We therefore look about to see where we may meet with this Supply, and Material Beings with which we're compass'd do first present themselves. These are the Objects of our Senses, it is at their presence that the Body tasts all its Pleasures, no wonder therefore if it endeavour to persuade us that our Good is here, tho a little Consideration, if not our frequent disappointments when we seek no further, were sufficient one wou'd think to convince us that it is not. For when we come to weigh 'em in an impartial

Consideration we discern, that as they are GOD's Work they have a Perfection suitable to their several Natures, and are as perfect as is consistent with the several Ranks and Stations they are plac'd in, so that consider'd Positively they are not to be Contemn'd, since they set forth the Wisdom, Power and Goodness of their Maker. But if we compare them with the Human Soul they appear of little value, and of none at all in comparison of Him who made them; and since their Nature is beneath, and their Worth much less than ours, we cannot find our Happiness in 'em. They contribute 'tis true to the Preservation and Ease of the Body, they help to make it fit for the Service of the Mind; But since a very few of 'em will do this, the rest are but a load and trouble, so far from being useful, that they indeed hurt us, unless they're made to minister to Charity and Contemplation.

Let then these little things be drawn aside, these Clouds that hide the most adorable Face of GOD from us, these Mud-walls that enclose our Earthly Tabernacle and will not suffer us to be pierc'd with the Beams of his Glory, and wounded, not to Death but Life, with the Arrows of his Love and Beauty. In him we find that infinite Good which alone can satisfie us, and which is not to be found elsewhere! Somewhat in which we lose our selves with Wonder, Love and Pleasure! Somewhat too ineffable to be nam'd, too Charming, too Delightful not to be eternally desir'd! And were we not sunk into Sense, and buried alive in a croud of Material Beings, it might seem impossible to think of any thing but Him. For whether we consider the Infinite Perfection of his Nature, or the Interest we have in, and our intire dependance on him. Whether we consider him as Maker and Governor of all things, as filling all places, intimately acquainted with all Events, as Righteous in all his ways, and holy in all his works. Whether we contemplate his Almighty Power; or what seems more suitable to our Faculties and Condition, the Spotless Purity of his Nature, the Moral Rectitude of his Will, which guided by Infallible Wisdom always Chuses what is Best. And more particularly his Infinite Goodness, his Beneficence to the Children of Men; that he is not only Good in himself, but that he is also *Our* Good, the only Amiable Being, who is altogether Lovely, and worthy of All our Love, the Object of our Hope, the Sum of our Desire, the Crown of our Joy, without whom we shall for ever Languish and Grieve; Enjoying whom we have nothing to Fear, nor any thing to Hate but what wou'd deprive us of that Enjoyment. If we consider how much he has done to render us capable of this Happiness even when we fled from it; what affronts he has put up, with what Patience he bears our Follies and solicits our Return, in a Word, all the Wonders of his Love in Christ Jesus! We cannot sure do less than fix our Thoughts for ever on Him, and devote our selves Intirely to Him! All our Passions will be Charm'd, and every Inclination attracted! We shall no more dispute his Will, nor seek exemption from it, but with all Sincerity of Heart, and ardent Desire cry out, *Lord what wilt thou have me to do? Not my Will Lord, but thine be done!* The business of our Lives will be to improve our Minds and to stretch our Faculties to their utmost extent, that so we may have the fullest enjoyment our Nature will admit, of this ever satisfying and yet ever desirable, because an Infinite, and our True, Good.

As to what is to be done by way of Exercise, not to enter too far into the Philosophy of the Passions, suffice it briefly to observe: That by the Oeconomy of Nature such and such Motions in the Body are annext in such a manner to certain Thoughts in the Soul, that unless some outward force restrain, she can produce them when she pleases barely by willing them; and reciprocally several Impressions on the Body are communicated to, and affect the Soul, all this being perform'd by the means of the Animal Spirits. The Active Powers of the Soul, her Will and Inclinations are at her own dispose, her Passive are not, she can't avoid feeling Pain or other sensible Impressions so long as she's united to a Body, and that Body is dispos'd to convey these Impressions. And when outward Objects occasion such Commotions in the Bloud and Animal Spirits, as are attended with those Perceptions in the Soul which we call the Passions, she can't be insensible of or avoid 'em, being no more able to prevent these first Impressions than she is to stop the Circulation of the Bloud, or to hinder Digestion. All she can do is to Continue the Passion as it was begun, or to Divert it to another Object, to Heighten or to let it Sink by degrees or some way or other to Modifie and Direct it. The due performance of which is what we call *Vertue*, which consists in governing Animal Impressions, in directing our Passions to such Objects, and keeping 'em in such a pitch, as right Reason requires.

By which it appears that it is not a fault to have Passions, since they are natural and unavoidable, and useful too; for as the Inclinations are the Wings of the Soul, so these give Life and Vigor to the Inclinations, by disposing the Body to act according to the Determination of the Mind. But the fault lies here, we suffer 'em too often to get the Mastry of the Mind, to hurry it on to what Objects they please and to fix it there, so that it is not able to consider any Idea but what they present. Whereas the Soul can if she please, and if she makes use of her Authority in time, divert the Course of the Spirits, and direct 'em to a new Object, by Limiting or Extending her Ideas, and by laying aside those the Passions excited, and entertaining new ones. Nay, if we do but forbear to revolve such Considerations as are apt to continue the Commotion of the Spirits, it will cease of it self. This is what we *can* and *ought* to do, and if we do not perform it, we act rather like the Slaves of Sense than Creatures endued with Reason; but if we do, we can hardly receive any Injury from the Passions.

The way therefore to Govern 'em is to be always in a Temper fit for this, Recollect and Compos'd, holding our Minds in as even a poise as ever we can between Mirth and Melancholy, one of which Stupifies the Soul and the other Dissolves it; and both of 'em weaken and dispose it for Passion. Nothing but what feeds the ill humor will make Impression whilst it is under the power of *this*, nor any useful thing stay in it, but it lies open to all manner of evil, when it is violently agitated by *that*. Too much of either rendring us unfit to Converse with our selves or others; such a mixture of both as makes us Serious without Sourness, and Chearful without Levity, being the happy Temper. It is by surprize that the Passions injure us, they violently attack our Reason when she is not prepar'd to receive them, so that the Will is determin'd all of a sudden by Confuse Perceptions and Sensations. Nor is it easie to repulse them when once they have gain'd ground, because they often bribe our Guard, and get the Mastry of us by those very Considerations which shou'd have been arm'd against 'em. But Recollection, a sedate and sober frame of Mind, prevents this Mischief, it keeps our Reason always on her Guard and ready to exert her self; it fits us to Judge truly of all occurences, and to draw advantage from whatever happens. This is the true Art of Prudence, for that which properly speaks us Wise, is the accommodating all the Accidents of Life to the great End of Living. And since the Passiveness of our Nature makes us liable to many Sufferings which we cou'd wish to avoid, Wisdom consists in the using those Powers, which GOD has given us the free disposal of, in such a manner, as to make those very things which befal us against our Will, an occasion of Good to us.

For if we do not live like Machines, but like Reasonable Creatures, that is if we Observe, Examine and Apply whatever comes under our Cognizance, every Turn in our own and our Neighbours Life will be Useful to us. It is not to be deny'd that we're generally Critical Observators on our Neighbours, but I'm afraid it is with an Ill not a Good Design. We do't to feed our Pride by an ungenerous insulting over their Infirmities, or thinking to Excuse and Justifie our own Faults by theirs. But we seldom set a mark on the Precipices from whence they fell that we may avoid 'em, or note their False Steps, that ours may be more Exact.

And indeed as things are usually manag'd, since Modesty, Breeding, or Sheepish Cowardise, restrains even those who are capable of bettering Conversation, from Edifying Discourses, the only use we can make of that Time which the World borrows of us and Necessary Civility exacts, is to lay in Matter of Observation. I do not mean that we shou'd make Ill-natur'd Remarks, or Uncharitable Reflections on Particular Persons, but only that we take notice of the several workings of Human Nature, the little turns and distinctions of Various Tempers; there being somewhat peculiar almost in every one, which cannot be learn'd but by Conversation and the Reflections it Occasions. For as to the main, we learn it by looking into our own Hearts, one Person being but the Counterpart of another, so that they who thorowly Know themselves have a right Idea of Mankind in general, and by making reasonable allowances for Circumstances, may pretty well guess at Particulars.

But even the Knowledge of our selves is not to be had without the Temper here recommended. For since the Passions do mostly depend on the Constitution of the Body, Age, Education and way of Living; so that the same Object does not only Affect several Persons differently, but variously moves the very same Person at several Seasons; and there was once a time perhaps, when that which puts us now in a ferment had no power to move us: We must therefore to the general consideration of Human Nature already spoken of, add a more minute inquiry into our own; Observing our Particular Passions, that especially to which we're most inclin'd by Nature, on which all the rest in a manner depend; and all the Peculiarities that are to be found in our own Temper. Very great things many times depending on a trivial Humour; nor is it so often Reason, as our particular way of using it that determines our Thoughts and Actions. Now nothing less than a continual Watch and Application can procure us a sufficient Acquaintance with our selves, we cannot well discern what Objects most sensibly touch us; which is our weakest side; by what means it is Expos'd or Strengthened; how we may Restrain or rightly Employ a Passion we cou'd not Prevent; and consequently grow strong by our very Infirmities, whilst we make them an occasion of Exercising and Encreasing our Vertue; unless we're always in a watchful Frame, unless we make Remarks even whilst the Passion is working, and Constantly attend the least beatings of our own Heart. Our own Heart which is indeed one of the best Books we can Study, especially in respect of Morality, and one principal Reason why we're no better Proficients in useful Knowledg, is because we don't duly consult it.

Again, we shou'd endeavour to render Spiritual and Future things as Present and Familiar as may be, and to withdraw as much as we can from sensible Impressions, especially from such as attack us violently. She whose Mind is busied about the former will find 'em of Weight and Moment sufficient to employ all her Passions, whilst the other will be scarce taken notice of; or be look'd on with Indifferency, because they appear to deserve very little Admiration, Joy, or Sorrow, and are not of value enough to discompose the Mind. And tho we have not Ambition to aspire to St. *Paul's* Perfection, who was *Crucified to the World and the World to him*, a greater Character than that of *Universal Monarch*; tho we think it impossible to be wholly Insensible to it whilst we live in it: Yet sure we can't deny that it is Possible, and very much our Duty, to be more indifferent to the Objects of Sense than the most of us are. For we certainly do amiss if we fix our Eyes and Thoughts so constantly on 'em, as that at last we take them for the most considerable things, and imagine that our Happiness is here; or, tho we can't be so gross as to *believe* this, yet if we *act* as if we did; it wou'd become us much better to argue, that the Possession of these Worldly Advantages which Mankind so much contend for, is Good if it can procure us Eternal Felicity; and that the Want of 'em is an Evil, if it exclude us from the Kingdom of Heav'n.

By which we learn how necessary it is to Retire and Meditate frequently; and how much it becomes us to keep out of the way of Theatrical Shows and inordinate Merriments, and not so much as to enter into a Parley with those Pomps and Vanities we renounc'd in our Baptism. For tho some extraordinary Tempers may make use of these to stir up the Powers of their Soul, and to give them a greater aversion to Vanity, as some Poysons are said to be Antidotes against others, yet for the most part they have an ill Effect: Because they deprive the Soul of real Joy and divine Serenity, by making too strong an Impression on the Senses, whereby the Animal Spirits are very much Mov'd and Exhausted, and being spent on trifles the Mind is left Dull, Unactive, and Melancholy too, especially if it Reflect on its Actions as it ought; so natural and necessary is it, that Vain Mirth shou'd conclude in Heaviness.

Again, the Passions consider'd as Bodily Impressions only, excite us many times to the Gratification of the Animal in prejudice of the Rational Nature. For tho Mankind had Originally no Appetites but what might Innocently be satisfied; yet since our Degeneracy, and that we have lost the true Relish of Good and Evil, they often give us false alarms, stirring us up to Pursue or Avoid what indeed we Ought not, if we consult our Good in the Main, and not the pleasing of a Part, nay the worst part of us. But if we consider 'em as attending our Inclinations, they can do no hurt, let 'em be as Brisk and Active as they can, provided they fix on their Proper Objects. Now what these are is to be found by the Nature of the Passions, by which we are led to the Use of 'em, since every thing ought to be employ'd about that which it is fitted for. But this being already accounted for by *Des Cartes* and *Dr. More*, in his excellent *Account of Vertue.* I cannot pretend to add any thing to what they have so well Discours'd. Only as a further confirmation of what has been already said we may observe; That Admiration gives Rise to

Les Passions de l' Amo.

144

all the Passions; for unless we were Affected with the Newness of an Object, or some other remarkable Circumstance, so as to be attentively engag'd in the Contemplation of it, we shou'd not be any wise mov'd, but it wou'd pass by unregarded. And therefore 'tis very necessary not to be struck with *little* things, or to busie our Minds about 'em, but to fix all our Attention on, and to keep all our Admiration for things of the greatest moment, such as are those which relate to another World.

We may further observe, that there is a leading Passion almost in every one, to which the Temper of their Body inclines, and on which the rest do in a manner wholly depend, especially if it be confirm'd by Education and Custom, so that if we duly manage *this*, we have the Command of all. Some are more subject to *Fear*, some to *Hope*, to *Joy*, *Sorrow* or the like, than others; but *Love* seems to be the predominant Passion in every one, and that which makes one of the former more remarkable than another, is only because it has been oftner mixt with Love. And indeed, since this is at the bottom of all the Passions, one wou'd think they're nothing else but different Modifications of it, occasion'd by some Circumstance in the Subject or Object of this Passion. Thus *Desire* is a Love to Good consider'd as Future; *Hope* the Passion that diposes us to believe we may, and *Fear* that we shall not obtain it. *Joy* is a pleasant Commotion of the Soul in the Fruition of the Good we Love; and *Sorrow* a disagreeable one occasion'd by the want of it, or presence of its contrary. The like may be said of the rest, for even *Hatred* tho it appear directly opposite to Love, may be refer'd to it, the very same motion that carrys the Soul towards Good, carrying her also from those things which wou'd deprive her of it, which on that account are call'd Evils, and why do we Hate any thing, but because it does some way or other hinder our Enjoyment of what we Love?

If therefore our Love be Right, the rest of our Passions will of course be so; and our Love which is *a motion of the Soul to joyn it self to that which appears to be grateful to it,* will then be right when our Notions of Good and Evil are; That is, when we do not take up with Imaginary or Particular, but pass on to the Sovereign Good, to GOD who is the only proper and adequate Object of our Love, as Sin is of our Hatred, all things else being no otherwise to be Pursued or Avoided, than in proportion to the Relation they bear to these. So that if we Love GOD with *All* our Soul, as He certainly Deserves, and as we certainly Must if we wou'd be Happy; we shall be so taken up with the Contemplation and *Admiration* of his Beauties, have so boundless an *Esteem,* such an awful *Veneration* for, and so great a *Contempt* of all things in Comparison of Him; that our *Desires* will be carried out after nothing but GOD, and such things as may further our Union with Him. His Favour, and the Light of His Countenance will be the Object of our *Hopes,* nor shall we much *Fear* any thing but His Displeasure. No *Grief* will pierce our Heart but for our many Offences against, and our Imperfect *Enjoyment of Him.* *We shall perfectly Hate all evil ways,* be *Jealous* of Sin at the remotest distance, and *suspect* every thing that has the least appearance of a Temptation. We shall be extremely Watchful over all our Actions, and never Resolve upon any till we're fully assur'd it is conformable to his Will and Pleasure. Whither will not our *Emulation* rise, what Difficulties won't our *Courage* surmount, when th'Enjoyment of a GOD is what we aspire to! The defects of our Services, and our failings in our Duty towards Him, will be the only occasion of *Shame;* for Reproach from Men when suffer'd for His sake will be counted a high Encomium, and his Approbation our only *Glory.* If ever we are *Angry* it will be when His Laws are Contemn'd and Right Reason violated; a just *Indignation* will arise when the Worthless are Prefer'd, and Merit is left unregarded. His Favourites will be ours, we shall dispense our *Good will* to every one proportionably as they are dear to Him; and shall think our *Gratitude* can never enough express it self, to that Bountiful Being from whom we receiv'd our All. And Oh! with what *Joy* and *Satisfaction of Mind* shall we proceed in every step of this! how pure and exalted is that Pleasure, how highly entertaining, which results from the right use of our Faculties, and Fruition of the Sovereign Good! Happiness is the natural Effect as well as the Reward of an Ardent Love to GOD, and what necessarily flows from it, Universal Piety: That Holy Soul is always serene, and full of unutterable Bliss, whose Reason Directs, and whose Passions readily Obey, whilst both are Guided by his Will and Spirit who is Infallible. She tasts a Pleasure which the World can neither give nor take away, nor can Worldly Minds so much as Imagine it: She is satisfied with the Past, Enjoys the Present, and has no Solicitude for, but a Joyful Expectation of what's approaching. For why the Dawnings of a Blisful Endless Day, break forth already in that Happy Mind, whose Temper and Constitution is Heavenly; it has a Foretaste, and thereby a well-grounded Assurance, of never-ceasing Joys to Come!

So far (by the way) is Religion from being an Enemy either to Nature or Pleasure, that it perfects the one, and raises the other to the greatest height. It teaches us the true Use of the Creatures, keeps us from expecting more in them than we can ever find, and leads us to the Enjoyment of the Creator who only can satisfie us. For I wou'd fain know of any experienced Person, whether any of the Delights of this World did ever answer Expectation when Enjoy'd, and whether the Joys of Religion do not exceed it? We come to the first with mighty hopes and are always Disappointed, to the last we approach with Fear and Trembling, supposing it will rob us of all the Satisfactions of Life, we shrink at the Pain and Difficulty, and thats the only thing in which after a little Trial we find our selves much mistaken. Good Christians being indeed the truest *Epicures,* because they have the most tastful and highest Enjoyment of the greatest Good.

For GOD is too Kind and Bountiful to deny us any Pleasure befitting our Nature; he does not require us to relinquish Pleasure, but only to exchange the Gross and Insipid for the Pure and Relishing, the Pleasures of a Brute for those of a Man. He wou'd not have us enslav'd to any Appetite, or so taken up with any Created Good whatever, as not to be able to maintain the Empire of our Reason and Freedom of our Will and to quit it when we see occasion. And this is all that the Rules of Self-Denial and Mortification tend to so far as they are Rational, they mean no more than the procuring us a Power and Disposition to do that which we come now in the last place to recommend, which is, To sanctifie our very Infirmities, to make even the disorderly Commotions of our Spirits an occasion of producing Holy Passions. It were better indeed if they were rais'd upon a right Principle; that the Passions did not move the Mind, but the Mind the Passions; and that the Motives to Religion were not Sensitive but Rational. However in the Infancy of our Vertue, it may not be amiss to make some use of our

Vices, and what we advise if it serve no other end, 'twill help
at least to break Ill-Habits and that's a considerable benefit.

Ladies'
Calling. Agreeable to which did an excellent Author bespeak the Ladies
sometime ago: *Let her that is Amorous, place her Love upon*
him who is the Chiefest among ten thousand; she that is Angry
turn her edg against her Sins; she that is haughty disdain the
Devils Drudgery; she that is Fearful dread him who can destroy,
both Body and Soul in Hell; and she that is sad reserve her Tears
for her Penitential Offices. Which, with the rest of that Authors
Ingenious and Kind Advice, I heartily wish were not only to
be seen in their Closets, but transcrib'd in their Hearts and Legi-
ble in their Lives and Actions.

Now in order to this, if our guard has been surpriz'd, and
some sensible Impression has strongly broke in upon us, so that
we find our selves all in a ferment, let us manage the Opportunity
discreetly, change the Object and hallow the Passion. Which is
no very difficult thing, for when a Passion is boyling it will
spend it self on any Object that we please to fix it on. And the
Proper Objects of our Passions, being most considerable in
'emselves, and naturally most apt to move us if we'll but give
them fair play, that is allow 'em a place in our Thoughts, they'll
work out the other, and make our Passions what they shou'd be:
We have a plain Instance of this in Afflictions, in which our
Grief is at first excited by some outward Cause, and when
that has softned us, the Spirit of GOD who is never wanting
unless we Neglect or Quench him, improves this Worldly into
a *Godly Sorrow* that worketh Repentance not to be Repented of.

Besides, as there is a Pleasure in the Passions as well as in
all the genuine Operations of Nature, so there's a Pain accompanying 'em when misplac'd, which disposes the Mind to a readiness
to rectifie them, that so it may enjoy the Pleasure without mixture
of Pain. If therefore we assist it with a little Meditation, it will
readily come over; and tho we may find it difficult absolutely
to quash a Passion that is once begun, yet it is no hard matter
to transfer it, so that it may pour forth it self in all its pleasing
transports, without fear of danger, or mixture of uneasiness.

But a Caution will not be amiss, which is, that we don't
mistake the Fits of Passion for a Spirit of Piety and Devotion.
They are good beginnings 'tis true, but if we're only wafted
up to Heaven in our Closets, and shew forth nothing or very

little of it in our Lives and Conversations, we may cheat our selves with the conceit of being Holy, but neither GOD nor Man will be so impos'd on. She who mourns for her Sins, tho never so bitterly, and yet returns to them at the next occasion, gives a very good Evidence of her Weakness, but none of her Repentance. She who pretends to never so great transports of Love to GOD, and yet is wedded to the world, can part with nothing for his sake, nor be content and easie when He only is her Portion, gives Him good words, and makes Him many fine Complements and that's the whole of the matter. She who makes shew of great Awe and Reverence towards the Divine Majesty at Church and has no regard to Him in the World his larger Temple, as good as declares that she thinks his Presence confin'd to a place, or that she hopes to commute a Days neglect for an Hours Observance, and expresses her Contempt of GOD much more than her Veneration. How can she profess to Hope in Him who is Anxious and Solicitious about the least Event? Or say that her Desires are fix't on GOD who has a great many Vanities and Sensual Apetites to be Satisfied?

Nor are we less out of the way when we tincture our Religion with our Passions, and fashion an Idea of it according to our own Complection not the tenor of the Gospel. Hence comes that great diversity we meet with both in Practice and Theory, for as there is somewhat Peculiar almost in every ones Temper, so is there in their Religion. Is our Disposition Sad and Cloudy, are we apt to take Offence, Suspicious and hard to be pleas'd? we imagine GOD is so, Religion is not our Joy but our Task and Burden, we became extremely scrupulous and un-easie to our selves and others. And if Resolution and Daring be joyn'd with our Melancholy, and Temptations fall pat in our way, we discard such a troublesome Religion and set up for Atheism and Infidelity. On the other hand, if we're Fearful and Timerous our Superstition has no bounds, we pay less regard to those Laws our Maker has prescrib'd, than we do to those Chimera's our own Fancy has invented to reconcile Him. A mistake which the Brisk and Jovial are sensible of, but not of the contrary extreme they run into; they discern that GOD's ways are ways of Pleasantness, and all his Paths are Peace, that Good Christians live the Happiest Lives, 'tis their Duty to Rejoyce evermore, and all the good things of the World are at their service. All which is very true, but then it is as true, that their Pleasures are not Sensual but Rational and Spiritual, which is not a lessening, but an Addition to their Character; that we are to Use the World so as not to abuse either our selves or it, to testify on all occasions our Moderation and Contempt of it, to be ready to quit it, nay even to part with Life it self when ever they come in competition with our Duty. In a word, if our Anger against our own Sins provokes us to be Peevish with others, tho not so good as they shou'd be, it goes too far. If our Zeal finds fault with all who do not come up to our Heights, or who don't express their Devotion in our way, it is not according to Knowlege, that is, it is not Discreet and Christian. If our great Love to GOD takes us up so much, that we think we may be morose and ill-natur'd to our Neighbour, we express it in a very disagreeable way: And I dare say it wou'd be more acceptable to Him, if instead of spending it all in Rapture and Devotion, a part of it were employ'd in Imitating his Beneficence to our Fellow-Creatures.

To wind up all; The Sum of our Duty and of all Morality, is to have a Temper of Mind so absolutely Conform'd to the Divine Will, or which is the same in other words, such an Habitual and Intire Love to GOD, as will on all occasions excite us to the Exercise of such Acts, as are the necessary consequents of such a Habit. This frame and Constitution of Soul is what we must all our Life time Labour after, it is to be begun, and some Proficiency made in it whilst we stay on Earth, and then we may joyfully wait for its Consummation in Heaven, the reason why we cannot be perfectly Happy whilst we tarry here, being only because we can have this Temper but Imperfectly. The want of which is the Hell of the Damn'd, the degree of their misery bearing a proportion to their opposition to the Divine Will. For Happiness is not *without* us, it must be found in our own Bosoms, and nothing but a Union with GOD can fix it there; nor can we ever be United to Him any other wise than by being like Him, by an Intire Conformity to his Will.

Now she who has obtain'd this blessed Temper, whose Will is Right, and who has no Passion but for GOD's Service, is pleas'd that his Wisdom shou'd Chuse her Work, and only prepares to dispatch it with the greatest Diligence and Chearfulness. She keeps All his Precepts, and does not pick and Chuse such as are for her turn, and most agreeable to her own Humor; but as she does every thing for His Sake, so is she easy and pleas'd under all his Dispensations; is truly indifferent to Applause, and fully content with GOD's Approbation. Indeed the Conquest of our Vanity is one of our last Triumphs, and a Satisfaction in all GOD's Choices for us, from a full Conviction that they are most for our advantage, the best Test of a Regular Will and Affections. For these are heights to which we can't arrive till we have travers'd over all the Paths of Vertue, and when once our Passions are reduc'd to this, I know not in what they can oppose us.

Not but that we're strictly oblig'd to *Provide for honest things in the Sight of Men* as well as of GOD, to do nothing but what is of *Good Report; to Abstain from all Appearance of Evil;* not to *give Occasion* of Slander to those who desire and *Seek* it; but to *Let our Light so shine before Men, that they may see our Good-works and Glorify our Father who is in Heaven.* But when we have done this, and have taken all possible care to approve our selves to GOD and Man, can we be at Ease if we fail in the latter? Are we more desirous of a Good than a Great Reputation? and wou'd we not to get a Name amongst our Fellow Servants, do any thing that may in the least Offend, or be less acceptable to our Common Master? Can we bear the being Censur'd as Singular and Laugh'd at for Fools, rather than comply with the evil Customs of the Age? and are we much more Covetous of the Substance *Vertue,* than of the Shadow *Fame?* If it be so we're pretty sure that all is Right, and that GOD's will is the Rule, and his Glory the End of all our Actions. It goes to a good Womans heart to receive that Commendation which the good-nature or Civility of another bestows on her, when she knows she does not Merit it, and to find whilst she's applauded abroad, a thousand Follies, Mistakes and Weaknesses in her own Mind. All the use that she makes of her Credit and Esteem in the World, is to excite her to Deserve it, tho at present perhaps she does not, and *Really* to come up to that Character which all are Ambitious to have.

Again, what is said of Submission and a perfect acquiescence in the Divine Will, is not to be so understood as if it were a fault to change our Circumstances when we're fairly and honestly call'd to't, or that we might not seek by honourable ways to enlarge them if they fit too strait. But it is design'd to correct that Complaining humor, which makes us always dissatisfied with the Present, and longing after a Change; which, how Religious soever we wou'd appear, is a very sure sign that our Passions are not mortified nor our Will reduced to a due Regularity: As hers is without doubt who can be pleas'd when even her most innocent Desires are denied, when she is disappointed in what she thinks her Best Designs. For such an one has nothing in her Temper that Sensible Impressions can so strongly fasten on, as to discompose her Mind; and what can she meet with to seduce her to Unlawful, who desires not to be her own Chuser in Lawful and Indifferent things?

The Laws of GOD have a Natural and Inward Goodness, which wou'd recommend them to a Rational Mind tho they were not injoyn'd, and therefore no wonder that Temper inclines one, Conveniency another, and Reputation a third to the Practise of some of them. But a Will duly regulated passes over these and is acted by a higher Motive, she who is Religious upon a Right Principle regards the Will of GOD only, for that and that alone is able to carry her Uniformly and Constantly thro all her Duty. Thus Acts of Beneficence, Liberality and Charity, are full of Lustre, they procure for their Possessor a lofty Character, and therefore whether we Value them or no, we're willing however to *seem* to be fond of 'em. We fancy what mighty things we wou'd do were we in such or such a Persons Circumstances, and long to be Rich and Great that we may Relieve the Needy and Rescue the Oppressed. But we are not so forward in aspiring after Poverty, tho nothing shews a Braver Mind than the bearing it Nobly and Contentedly; we care not to be the Oppressed Person, that we might exercise Meekness and Forgiveness, Patience and Submission. Not but that the Vertues of Adversity are as lovely in themselves, and as Acceptable to GOD as those of Prosperity, or rather more so, because they express a greater Love to GOD, are more opposite to Vicious Self-Love, and do more eminently declare the Veneration we have for the Divine Wisdom and Goodness, which we can Adore and Delight in, which we can Justify and Applaud even in the most uneasy Circumstances. But they don't make so great a Figure in the World, they don't feed our Vanity so much, nor are so agreeable to Flesh and Bloud, and that's the reason why we care not for them.

Tis true we profess that we desire Riches and Honour, a great Reputation and Theater in the World, on not other account but to do GOD Service. But if we are real in this, why don't we perform so much as we might in our present Station? Alas! we Cheat our selves, as well as endeavour to impose on others; and under Pretence of seeking GOD's Glory, in Reality pursue nothing but our own. For had we indeed that Esteem for GOD and Intire Conformity to his Will, which is at once both the Duty and Perfection of all Rational Beings, we shou'd not complain of his Exercise of that Power, which a Prince or even an Ordinary Master has a Right to; which is, to set his Servants about such work as he thinks them fittest for. If we allow that GOD Governs the Universe, can we so much as imagine that it is not Govern'd with the Greatest Justice and Equity, Order and Proportion? Is not every one of us plac'd in such Circumstances as Infinite Wisdom discerns to be most suitable, so that nothing is wanting but a careful observation whither they lead us, and how we may best improve them? What reason then to complain of the Management of the world? and indeed except in the Morals of Mankind which are visibly and grossly deprav'd, I see not why we shou'd so much as wish for any alteration. The Wicked Prosper sometimes and what then? shall we grudge them their Portion *here*, since that's their All, and alas a very sorry one!

Besides, this world is not a soil for perfect Happiness to Grow in, Good and Evil are blended together, every Condition has its Sweet and Bitter, we may be Made by Adversity and ruin'd by Prosperity according as we manage them. Riches and Power put opportunities of doing Good into our hands, if we have a Will to Use them, but at the same time they furnish us with Instruments of doing Evil. They afford us at once the Conveniencies of Life and fuel for irregular Appetites. They make us known to others, but many times hinder us from being acquainted with our selves. They set us in view, so that if our Example be Bright it becomes the more Illustrious; but we must also remember that our Faults are as conspicuous as our Vertues, and that Peoples eyes are most intent on *those*, and most inquisitive to find 'em, so that even our innocent Liberties are many times misconstrued.

By Obscurity, and a Narrow Fortune, we're depriv'd of somewhat Necessary or Commodious to our Present Living, but are quickned to a more diligent concern for a Life to Come; we don't find our Good things *here*, and common Prudence will teach us to take care that we may enjoy them *hereafter*. If we do not Possess much, we have not much to Lose, nor such great Accounts to make; have little Business and less Authority with others, but hereby the more Command of our own Time and Thoughts. Our Vertue is plac'd in an ill-light, and our Wisdom rejected with a *What Impertinents are these, who pragmatically attempt to Instruct their Betters?* but we have fewer Temptations to shock the one, and greater Advantages, as things are commonly manag'd to improve both. We're expos'd to the Contempt and Outrage of the World, but that makes us less in love with it, and more ready to welcome Death, whene're it brings the kind Releasing Summons.

It may be thought a considerable omission that no directions have bin given, any further than the management of our *Own* Inclinations and Passions; tho't be very advantageous to know how to deal with other Peoples, both in regard of Education, and of the Influence that they have on ours. But I have this to say, that Education is a beaten Subject, and has been accounted for by better Pens than mine: And that in this as in all other things, we are to treat our Neighbours as we do our selves, shew 'em the unsuitableness of those Objects which Irregular Affections pursue, and persuade them to a willing use of such methods as we take to Cure our own. It requires I confess, no little Skill to do this to purpose, and to convince them that we're really their Friends, whilst we strive to divorce them from such Objects as they're endear'd and fastned to by a thousand tyes: And this is so nice a matter, so laborious a task, that the more I consider it the more unable I find my self to give fit Directions for the performance of it. They who wou'd do that, must have a more exact Knowlege of Human Nature, a greater Experience of the World, and of those differences which arise from Constitution, Age, Education, receiv'd Opinions, outward Fortune, Custom and Conversation, than I can pretend to. And perhaps there is no need of Directions since few will attempt to practise them; for if a Passion that is young and tender gives us work enough, as the difficulty of Education plainly shews it does, they had need be very Kind, very Good, and very Wise, who set about the Cure of an Old and inveterate one. Nor can they who have so much Divinity in their Mind as to design such a noble work, be thought to stand in need of any advice how to perform it.

However, I'le venture to say in general, that we must never oppose Commotion with Commotion nor be in Passion our selves if we wou'd reform anothers, else we lose many good Opportunities and seem to seek the gratification of our own humor rather than our Neighbours good. No discouragements shou'd shock us, no ungrateful returns shou'd sower our Temper, but we must expect and be prepar'd to bear many repulses and wild disorders, and patiently sustain that greatest uneasiness to a Christian Mind, the bitter appearance that our Hopes are lost, and that all the Labour of our Love is ineffectual! We must abound both in Good-Nature and Discretion, and not seldom make use of quite contrary Means to bring about the End we aim at. Removing all Fuel from the Passion sometimes; and sometimes Indulging it as far as Innocently we may; and if nothing else will do, give it line enough, that so it may destroy it self in its own Excesses.

But ah! will any one drive us to such a desperate Remedy as often Kills, and cannot Cure without a very great Care, and a more than Ordinary assistance of GOD's Grace, which they have little reason to hope for, who abandon themselves to Temptations, and push things to such Extremities! Will nothing less than Temporal Ruin which unreasonable Passions naturally end in, serve to prevent Eternal and it were well if even that wou'd do, for they usually involve in both. If therefore such as are in Passion are capable of hearing any thing but what sooths 'em in their own way, I wou'd beg of 'em for GOD's sake and their own, to grant but this one very easy and equitable Request, which is Calmly to Hear and to Consider what may be said against their darling Passion. For if it be Right it will stand the test of all that can be urg'd against it; if it be not, is it Good for them to retain and cherish it any longer? And if they refuse to listen to the *Kind*, tho according to them, unseasonable and mistaken advice that is given, and seek no further than for Arguments to Justifie themselves, do they not by so great a Partiality secretly confess that they are in the Wrong, and wou'd not have it discover'd that they are so, because they're resolv'd with or without Reason to continue their irregular Passion?

And the cause of this strange Resolution seems to be this, That a Passion of any sort having got the hank of one, it becomes so Natural, so Agreeable, that the going about to wean them from it, looks like an attempt to deprive them of all their Joy; and they're hardly persuaded to part with what's a *Present* Delight, let its Consequences be what they may, and tho the quitting of it be in order to th' enjoyment of that much Sweeter, as well as Nobler Pleasure, which arises from the due use of Reason; and with which those Wise and Holy Souls are entertain'd, who prefer the relishes of a Rational before those of an Animal Life.

But they ought not to think us their Enemies, when we endeavour their Cure, tho we happen to Lance and Scarifie them. They who are Sick of Passion are like People in a Lethargy, insensible of their Danger; nay they're fond of their Disease, and set themselves against our Medicines; tho the greater unwillingness they show to be Disturb'd, so much the more need of Rousing 'em out of their pleasing slumber. The more secure they think themselves, the more wretched is their Condition, for that's a sign that the Passion has got an intire Possession of their Soul, and has fortified all its Avenues against Reason and Wholesome Advice. And 'tis worth being remarqued, that our Inclinations how Innocent and Harmless soever they appear, are always to be suspected if the Passions that accompany them are violent. For Violence does not Answer but Destroy the Use of Passion, it hinders th'Operations of the Soul, insted of disposing the Body to follow her Directions Vigorously.

And as to the Influence that another Persons Passion may have on us, enough has bin said to warn us, not to dally with the Flame when our Neighbours house is on Fire, lest we be consum'd in it; and carefully to avoid doing any thing which may excite, or encrease their Passions. But when we discern that the Plague is begun, let's remove with all possible speed out of the infected Air. Great Passions arise from very small beginings, and that which appear'd Innocent at first if allow'd on that account, does often become our Ruin, or gives us at least the greatest trouble in overcoming it.

The CONCLUSION

THUS you have Ladies, the best Method I can at present think of for your Improvement, how well it answers by Design the World must judge. If you are so favourable as to think it comes up to't in any measure, what remains but to put it in Practise, tho in the way in which you live, 'tis not probable that all of you either Will or Can, for reasons mention'd in the first Part, and particularly because of the great waste of your P. 28, &c. Time, without Redeeming of which there's nothing to be done. It is not my intention that you shou'd seclude your selves from the World, I know it is necessary that a great number of you shou'd live in it; but it is Unreasonable and Barbarous to drive you into't, e're you are capable of doing Good in it, or at least of keeping Evil from your selves. Nor am I so fond of my Proposal as not to lay it aside very willingly, did I think you cou'd be sufficiently serv'd without it. But since such Seminaries are thought proper for the Men, since they enjoy the fruits of those Noble Ladies Bounty who were the foundresses of several of their Colleges, why shou'd we not think that such ways of Education wou'd be as advantageous to the Ladies? or why shou'd we despair of finding some among them who will be as kind to their own Sex as their Ancestors have been to the other? Some Objections against this design have already been consider'd, and those which I have since met with are either too trifling to deserve a serious Answer, or too Ill-natur'd not to require a severer than I care to give them. They must either be very Ignorant or very Malicious who pretend that we wou'd imitate Foreign Monastries, or object against us the Inconveniencies that they are subject to; a little attention to what they read might have convinc'd them that our Instituion is rather *Academical* than *Monastic*. So that it is altogether beside the purpose, to say 'tis too Recluse, or prejudicial to an Active Life; 'tis as far from that as a Ladys Practising at home is from being a hindrance to her dancing at Court. For an Active Life consists not barely in *Being in the World, but in doing much Good in it:* And therefore it is fit we Retire a little, to furnish our Understandings with useful Principles, to set our Inclinations right, and to manage our' Passions, and when this is well done, but not till then, we may safely venture out.

As for those who think so Contemptibly of such a considerable part of GOD's Creation, as to suppose that we were made for nothing else but to Admire and do them Service, and to make provision for the low concerns of an Animal Life, we pity their mistake, and can calmly bear their Scoffs, for they do not express so much Contempt of us as they do of our Maker; and therefore the reproach of such incompetent Judges is not an Injury but an Honor to us.

The Ladies I hope pass a truer estimate on themselves, and need not be told that they were made for nobler purposes. For tho I wou'd by no means encourage Pride, yet I wou'd not have them take a mean and groveling Spirit for true Humility. A being content with Ignorance is really but a Pretence, for the frame of our nature is such that it is impossible we shou'd be so; even those very Pretenders value themselves for some Knowlege or other, tho it be a trifling or mistaken one. She who makes the most Grimace at a Woman of Sense, who employs all her little skill in endeavouring to render Learning and Ingenuity ridiculous, is yet very desirous to be thought Knowing in a Dress, in the Management of an Intreague, in Coquetry or good Houswifry. If then either the Nobleness or Necessity of our Nature unavoidably excites us to a desire of Advancing, shall it be thought a fault to do it by pursuing the best things? and since we *will* value our selves on somewhat or other, why shou'd it not be on the most substantial ground? The Humblest Person that lives has some Self-Esteem, nor is it either Fit or Possible that any should be without it. Because we always Neglect what we Despise, we take no care of its Preservation and Improvement, and were we throughly possess'd with a Contempt of our selves, we shou'd abandon all Care both of our Temporal and Eternal Concerns, and burst with Envy at our Neighbours. The only difference therefore between the Humble and the Proud is this, that whereas the former does not prize her self on some Imaginary Excellency, or for any thing that is not truly Valuable; does not ascribe to her self what is her Makers due, nor Esteem her self on any other account but because she is GOD's Workmanship, endow'd by him with many excellent Qualities, and made capable of Knowing and Enjoying the Sovereign and Only Good; so that her Self-Esteem does not terminate in her *Self* but in GOD, and she values her self only for GOD's sake. The Proud on the contrary is mistaken both in her Estimate of Good, and in thinking it is her Own; She values her self on things that have no real Excellency, or which at least add none to her, and forgets from whose Liberality she receives them: She does not employ them in the Donors Service, all her care is to Raise her self, and she little considers that the most excellent things are distributed to others in an equal, perhaps in a greater measure than to herself, they have opportunities of advancing as well as she, and so long as she's puft up by this Tumor of Mind, they do really excel her.

The Men therefore may still enjoy their Prerogatives for us, we mean not to intrench on any of their Lawful Privileges, our only Contention shall be that they may not out-do us in promoting his Glory who is Lord both of them and us; And by all that appears the generality will not oppose us in this matter, we shall not provoke them by striving to be better Christians. They may busy their Heads with Affairs of State, and spend their Time and Strength in recommending themselves to an uncertain Master, or a more giddy Multitude, our only endeavour shall be to be absolute Monarchs in our own Bosoms. They shall still if they please dispute about Religion, let 'em only give us leave to Understand and Practise it. And whilst they have unrival'd the Glory of speaking as *many* Languages as *Babel* afforded, we only desire to express our selves Pertinently and Judiciously in *One*. We will not vie with them in thumbing over Authors, nor pretend to be walking Libraries, provided they'll but allow us a competent Knowlege of the Books of GOD, Nature I mean and the Holy Scriptures: And whilst they accomplish themselves with the Knowlege of the World, and experiment all the Pleasures and Follies of it, we'll aspire no further than to be intimately acquainted with our own Hearts. And sure the Complaisant and Good natur'd Sex will not deny us this; nor can they who are so well assur'd of their own Merit entertain the least Suspicion that we shall overtop them. It is upon some other account therefore that they object against our Proposal, but what that is I shall not pretend to guess, since they do not think fit to speak out and declare it.

Some indeed are pleas'd to say, that tho this appears in Speculation to be a very Happy and Useful way of Living, it will be quite another thing when reduc'd to Practice. Variety of Humours will occasion Resentments and Factions, and perhaps other inconveniencies not yet foreseen; nor can we expect that every Person there will be of such an agreeable, obliging and teachable Temper, as neither to Give nor Take Offence. And supposing the first Company were as tractable and as happily cemented by the mutual love of Vertue, and prudent Management, as we cou'd desire, yet how can we be secure of their Sucessors, or that this as well as other good Institutions shall not degenerate?

I agree so far with this Objection as to grant that our Proposal is not such a piece of Perfection that nothing can be said against it, but is there any thing in this World that is so? Or do Men use to quit their Employments and Houses, their Wives and Children, Relations and Friends, upon every little pet, or because they very often find trouble or disagreeableness? do they not rather if they are good Christians, bear with Infirmities and endeavour to mend them? He then who wou'd Object to purpose must shew that the Good it may do is not equivalent to the Evil which may attend it; that the Ladies will suffer greater Inconveniencies with, than without it, and that it will not in the *Main* be best. Otherwise we shall take liberty to believe that it is Humor, Covetousness or any thing rather than Reason which restrains him from Approving and Promoting it. There is a certain Pride in the Mind of Man, which flatters him that he can See farther and Judge better than his Neighbour, and he loves to feed it by scrupling and objecting against what another proposes, who perhaps has not over-look'd those fine discoveries in which he hugs himself, but having view'd them on all sides has discern'd and despis'd their insignificancy. I wou'd only ask our Objectors whether they think the World so good as that it needs none, or so bad as that it is not capable of Amendment? If neither of these, let them tell me whether Complaining and Wishing will ever do the business, or who is the greatest Benefactor to Mankind, he who finds fault with every Project set on foot to better and improve them, because it is not exactly after the Pattern in the Mount, that is indeed according to his own tooth and relish; it is not beyond exception, but has a touch of Humane Weakness and Ignorance mingled with it? Or he who vigorously and sincerely with a pure heart and a diligent hand, sets about doing what he Can, tho not so much as he Wou'd, were his abilities greater? We're all apt enough to cry out against the Age, but to what purpose are our Exclamations unless we go about to Reform it? Not faintly and coldly as if we were unconcern'd for the success, and only wou'd do somewhat to still the reproaches of our Consciences and to exalt us in our own Imaginations, with the Pompous Idea of Zeal and Public Spiritedness; but *with all our Might*, with an Unwearied Industry and Vigor, I'me asham'd to say like that which the Instruments of Satan express in making Proselytes to Wickedness and Prophaneness; but rather with such as becomes the Servants of Christ, which bears some sort of proportion to the Greatness of our Master, the Importance of the Work and the Excellency of the Reward.

We do not expect that all who come into this Society will be perfect, but we will endeavour to make them and our selves so as much as may be. Nor shall any be admitted who either have not, or are not desirous to have, that Divine yet humble, that Great and Generous, yet Meek and Condescending Spirit, that unfeigned Love to GOD and all Mankind which was in Christ Jesus. We set no other Rules than those of the Gospel, Christianity being the highest Improvement of a Rational Nature, and every one's oblig'd to keep its Institutions whether they Live in such a Society or out of it.

And as for that degeneracy which it may fall into, 'tis too general an objection to have any weight, and may as well be urg'd against Universities, all sorts of Government, and indeed against every thing, as against this. *May be*'s and *if*'s are endless, and he who undertakes to provide against all Future Contingencies, either believes no GOD or fancies himself to be one. A Prudent Man will look as far as he can, and provide to the utmost of his Knowlege and Power, but when that's done, he knows he's but a Man and therefore can't possibly Forsee and Remedy all things.

Let's then do what we *Can*, and leave the rest to our Great Benefactor and Governor, but let us set about our own part, not only when the way is open and easy, who shall give us thanks for that? but in spite of all Difficulties and Discouragement, since we have so Glorious a Leader, so indefatigable in his Labours, so boundless in his Love, such an Omnipotent Assister who neither wants Power nor Will to help us. The Peevishness and Obstinacy of such as Quarrel with our Labour of Love and set themselves against all we can do to serve them, will only add to our Laurels and enlarge our Triumphs, when our Constancy in doing Good has at last o'ercome those Perverse Opposers of it.

The End.